The German Kitchen

Classic Dishes

Popular dishes from the Food Blog
my dinner.co.uk

Marita Sinden

table of CONTENTS

table of CONTENTS

hello there

Willkommen!

I'm excited to share with you my collection of favorite recipes from my food blog, mydinner.co.uk. The dishes in this cookbook were handpicked by my readers—recipes they felt were truly worth including in this special collection.

I'd love to say that I learned to cook as a child, but the truth is, it came out of necessity. When I left Germany to study in the UK, I suddenly missed all the comforting dishes I had grown up with. Red cabbage, potato dumplings, and currywurst were no longer easily available to me, so I had no choice but to learn how to make them from scratch.

Before long, I began documenting my cooking journey on my website, translating these beloved German recipes into English. And that's how the story of mydinner.co.uk began.

Inside this cookbook, you'll find tried-and-tested recipes from the blog. They are authentic German dishes, thoughtfully adapted for kitchens outside of Germany—with suggestions for ingredient substitutes when certain items are hard to find.

Whether you're brand new to German cooking or rediscovering family favorites, I hope these recipes bring joy to your table and stories to your home.

Viel Spass
Marita

Suppenküche

SOUPS

SERVING: 4 PEOPLE **PREP:** 15 MINS **COOK:** 1 HR 20 MINS

Gulaschsuppe

Goulash Soup

A favorite export from Hungary. We serve this soup often in winter during outdoor parties, like New Year's Eve, or at Mulled Wine Gathering with friends. It is filling and nutritious at the same time.

Ingredients

- 500 g (1 lb) stewing beef
- 2 tablespoons neutral oil (such as vegetable, sunflower, or avocado oil)
- 1 tablespoon butter
- 1 onion (approx. 120 g or 4.2 oz)
- 4 garlic cloves
- 1 tablespoon tomato paste
- 180 ml (¾ cup) dry red wine
- 1 liter (4 cups) beef broth

Spices

- 3 tablespoons sweet paprika powder
- 2 tablespoons hot paprika powder (optional)
- 1 teaspoon marjoram (or substitute with sage)
- 2 bay leaves
- 1 tablespoon granulated sugar

Soup Vegetables

- 3 large potatoes (350 g or 12 oz)
- 2 carrots (140 g or 5 oz)
- 2 peppers one red, yellow (140 or 5 oz)

Instructions

1. Prepare the meat by chopping it into 2 cm chunks. They should fit on a spoon. Peel and finely slice the onions and garlic.
2. Heat the butter and oil in a large saucepan and sear the beef on medium to high heat. It should brown on all sides to develop some roasting flavor. If you have a lot of meat, fry it in batches. Otherwise, the meat will cook rather than sear, and you will lose too much of the meat's juice. Remove the meat and set aside.
3. Add the onions and fry until they have browned. Then add the garlic and fry for a further minute.
4. Add the tomato paste, and fry for another further minute so it releases its roasting flavors. Add the meat back into the pot.
5. Deglaze the meat with the red wine and beef broth/stock and bring to a boil. Reduce the heat to medium-low. The soup should simmer rather than bubble wildly.
6. Add the seasonings: sugar, black pepper, sweet and spicy paprika powders (optional), marjoram, and bay leaves.
7. Cover the pan with the lid and cook the goulash soup on low to medium heat for 70 minutes.
8. In the meantime, peel, deseed, and chop the soup vegetables (potatoes, peppers, carrots) into bite-sized pieces.
9. Once the beef is cooked, add the vegetables to the soup and leave to boil for a further 20 minutes until the vegetables are tender.
10. Remove the soup from the heat, add more salt to taste, and add the finely chopped fresh parsley just before serving.

Find more images and tips at https://mydinner.co.uk/german-goulash-soup/ or Google *"MyDinner Goulash Soup"*.

SERVING: 6 PEOPLE **PREP:** 10 MINS **COOK:** 40 MINS

Linsensuppe

Lentil Soup

This hearty lentil soup is so comforting on cold winter days. Packed with lentils, vegetables, and a unique sweet and sour flavor, it is perfect for feeding a crowd.

Ingredients

- 150 g (5.2 oz) bacon
- 1 onion, about 120 g (5.2 oz)
- 1 tablespoon olive oil
- 250 g (9 oz) green or brown lentils
- 2 liters (8.5 cups) vegetable stock or broth
- 1 leek, whole stick, about 200 g (7 oz)
- 3 potatoes, about 450 g (1 lb)
- 2 carrots, about 200 g (7 oz)
- 1 teaspoon sugar
- Salt and pepper to taste
- 4 tablespoons white wine vinegar
- 3 sausages (Frankfurters or smoked sausages)
- Fresh bread, for serving

Instructions

1. Chop the bacon into small cubes. Peel and finely dice the onion.
2. Heat the olive oil in a large pot over medium heat. Sauté the bacon and onion until the onion becomes translucent.
3. Meanwhile, rinse the lentils thoroughly under cold running water. Add the lentils and the vegetable stock (or broth) to the pot. Bring to a gentle simmer and cook over medium to low heat for about 30 minutes. (*Adjust cooking time according to the instructions on your lentil package.)*
4. Slice the leek into thin rings. Peel the potatoes and carrots, then cut them into bite-sized cubes.
5. After the lentils have simmered, add the chopped leek, potatoes, and carrots to the pot. Continue cooking for another 10 minutes over medium heat.
6. Once the lentils and vegetables are tender, season the soup with salt, pepper, and a pinch of sugar. Stir in the vinegar, one tablespoon at a time, until it reaches your desired level of tanginess. If the soup is too thick, you can add more broth to adjust the consistency.
7. Turn off the heat. Place the sausages into the hot soup and let them warm through for about 5 minutes. The soup will cool slightly while the sausages heat up.
8. Serve the soup hot with a side of fresh bread.

SERVING: 4 PEOPLE **PREP:** 10 MINS **COOK:** 30 MINS

Bohnensuppe

Green Bean Soup

This recipe transforms simple ingredients into soul food. It's a rustic soup that is nourishing and satisfying. We often serve it in late summer when the beans are ripe in our garden. You can make this recipe with french or runner beans.

Ingredients

- 100 g (3.5 oz) smoked bacon
- 1 onion, about 120 g (4.2 oz)
- 4 carrots (about 350 g /12 oz)
- 4 potatoes (about 300 g / 10 oz)
- 1 liter (4 cups or 33 fl oz) beef or chicken broth/stock
- 2 smoked German sausages (e.g., Mettwurst), or substitute with Polish sausages like Krakauer or Kabanossi
- 500 g (1lb) green beans
- 1 tablespoon olive oil
- 1 teaspoon summer savory *(If unavailable, substitute with ¼ teaspoon sage and ½ teaspoon thyme)*
- Salt and pepper to taste

Instructions

1. Roughly cube the bacon, onion, carrots, and potatoes. Wash the green beans, trim the ends, and cut them into bite-sized lengths. Slice the sausages.
2. In a large stockpot, pour in the broth and add the carrots and potatoes. Bring to a boil and cook for about 10 minutes.
3. Stir in the green beans and continue cooking for another 15 minutes, or until all vegetables are tender.
4. Add the summer savory (or the sage and thyme substitute), and season with salt and pepper to taste.
5. Add the sliced sausages and let them heat through for a few minutes.
6. Serve hot with rye bread or a crusty roll.

More info at https://mydinner.co.uk/green-bean-soup/ or Google *"MyDinner Green Bean Soup"*.

SERVING: 4 PEOPLE   **PREP:** 10 MIN   **COOK:** 37 MIN

Kartoffelsuppe

Potato Soup

This is a staple at our house and we serve it as a main course. My children like it with frankfurter sausages, whereas my husband prefers it with smoked Mettwurst. Serve with bread and if desired a dollop of sour cream.

Ingredients

- 1 kg (2 lb 3 oz) potatoes – floury/starchy varieties like King Edward, Russet, or Yukon Gold
- 150 g (5 oz) root celery (celeriac) – optional
- 250 g (9 oz) leek – about 1 leek
- 150 g (5 oz) white onions – about 2 onions
- 150 g (5 oz) carrots – about 2 carrots
- 1 liter (34 fl oz or 4 cups) chicken stock or broth
- 1 teaspoon marjoram (or substitute with sage)
- 1 bay leaf
- 15 g (0.5 oz) fresh parsley, finely chopped
- 1 tablespoon olive oil
- 100 g (3.5 oz) heavy cream)
- Sausauges such as Frankfurters, Bratwurst, Kraukauer, Kielabasa, or Mettwurst

Instructions

1. Start by preparing the vegetables: Peel the potatoes, carrots, and celery root (if using), then cut them into small cubes. Peel and finely slice the onions. Cut the leek into thin strips. Finely chop the parsley.
2. Heat the olive oil in a large saucepan over medium heat. Add the onions and sauté until golden brown, about 5 minutes. Add the potatoes, leeks, celery root, and carrots, and sauté for another 2 minutes.
3. Pour in the broth/stock and add the bay leaf and marjoram. Cover with a lid and let simmer over medium-low heat for about 30 minutes, stirring occasionally. *(Note: The amount of salt needed depends on your broth. Season to taste.)*
4. Remove the pot from the heat. Check that the vegetables are cooked through and remove the bay leaf. For a creamy potato soup blend with a stand or immersion blender until you achieve a creamy consistency. Stir in the heavy cream or sour cream.
5. Adjust the seasoning with salt and black pepper to taste. Place the sausages into the warm (no longer cooking soup). The sausages (Frankfurters or smoked sausages such as Mettwurst) just need to be heated up, not cooked. Sprinkle in the fresh parsley just before serving.
6. If using bratwurst, slice it into small chunks and fry them in a little oil in a separate pan before adding to the soup.

More info at https://mydinner.co.uk/german-potato-soup/ or Google "*MyDinner Potato Soup*" .

SERVING: 4 PEOPLE **PREP:** 10 MINS **COOK:** 2 HRS

Erbsensuppe

Split Pea Soup

A recipe from my childhood, as we often served it at church gatherings. It is also a popular military dish, as it's economical and can be stretched to feed the masses.

Ingredients

- 250 g (1 cup / 9 oz) dried split peas
- 750 ml (3 cups / 25 fl oz) water
- 1 bay leaf
- 3 carrots (about 250 g / 9 oz), peeled and chopped into 1–2 cm (½ inch) cubes
- 3 potatoes (about 150 g / 9 oz), peeled and chopped into 1–2 cm (½ inch) cubes
- 1 leek (about 250 g / 9 oz), sliced into 1–2 cm (½ inch) rounds
- 150 g (5 oz) smoked bacon, diced
- 1 teaspoon marjoram (or substitute with sage)
- Salt and pepper to taste
- Fresh parsley, chopped (optional, for garnish)
- Sausages (optional, such as smoked sausage, kielbasa, or frankfurters)

Instructions

1. In a large pot, cook the split peas according to the package instructions with 750 ml (3 cups) of water and the bay leaf. It typically takes about 90 minutes until they are soft.
2. While the peas are cooking, peel and chop the carrots and potatoes into 1–2 cm (½ inch) cubes. Slice the leek into 1–2 cm (½ inch) rounds.
3. Once the split peas are fully cooked, add the chopped vegetables, diced bacon, and marjoram to the pot. Let the soup simmer for about 20 minutes, or until the vegetables are tender.
4. Season the soup with salt and pepper to taste. If using sausages, add them to the pot and let them warm through for about 5 minutes. Do not let them boil, as they may split
5. Just before serving, stir in the fresh parsley and check the seasoning one final time.
6. Serve hot with crusty rolls or rye bread.

More info at https://mydinner.co.uk/german-split-pea-soup-with-bacon/ or Google "*MyDinner Erbsensuppe*".

SERVING: 4 PEOPLE **PREP:** 20 MINS **COOK:** 1 HR 40 MINS

Hühnersuppe

Chicken Noodle Soup

This is a real classic soup. It's a great soup when you are feeling under the weather. Add as much vegetables to the soup as you want to. My children love this soup so much I make it in large batches and freeze it.

Ingredients

For the broth

- 1.5 kg (3.5 lb) whole chicken
- 2 teaspoons salt
- ½ leek (about 125 g / 4 oz)
- 2 carrots (about 150 g/5 oz)
- 1 onion (about 100 g)
- ¼ (about 150 g (5 oz)) celery root
- fresh parsley
- 1 teaspoon peppercorns
- 2 bay leaves

For the soup

- ½ leek (about 125 g / 4 oz) sliced
- 3 carrots (about 150 g/5 oz), peeled and chopped
- 300 g (2 cups) garden peas
- ⅓ head of cauliflower, (300 g, 10 oz) chopped
- 100 g (1 cup) German soup noodles, (or small pasta of choice)
- fresh parsley leaves

Instructions

1. Rinse the chicken under running water, then place it in a large pot. Cover with approximately 2.5 liters (11 cups) of water and add 2 teaspoons of salt. Bring to a boil, skimming off the froth or scum that forms on the surface. This step helps ensure a clear soup.
2. Peel the onion and roughly chop the broth vegetables, parsley, bay leaves, and peppercorns. Add them to the pot with the chicken and let the soup simmer uncovered for approximately 90 minutes, intermittently skimming off any scum that rises to the surface.
3. Meanwhile, peel and chop the carrots, cauliflower, and leeks (or any vegetables of your choice) into bite-sized pieces.
4. After the cooking time, remove the chicken from the pot and set it aside to cool slightly. Strain the broth through a fine-mesh sieve or cheesecloth to remove the vegetable solids, bay leaves, and peppercorns, then return the clear broth to the pot.
5. Once the chicken has cooled, remove the meat from the carcass, discarding the skin, excess fat, and any gristle. Roughly chop the meat into bite-sized pieces and return it to the pot.
6. Add the fresh vegetables and peas to the broth and simmer until tender, about 10–15 minutes.
7. In a separate pot, cook the soup noodles (or pasta of your choice) until al dente. Add the noodles to the soup just before serving. (If you plan to store leftovers, it's best to keep the noodles separate, as they can become mushy if left in the broth for too long.) Before serving, sprinkle the soup with fresh parsley.

More info at at https://mydinner.co.uk/german-chicken-soup/ or Google "*MyDinner Chicken Soup*".

SERVING: 4 PEOPLE **PREP:** 20 MINS **COOK:** 1 HR

Kohlsuppe

Cabbage Soup

A hearty, comforting cabbage soup that is delicious, budget-friendly, and easy. A power food for cold days and simple to make.

Ingredients

- 1 kg (2.2 lb) green or white cabbage
- 2 onions (200 g / 7 oz), finely chopped
- 1 clove garlic, minced
- 3 carrots (250 g / 9 oz), peeled and chopped
- 3 potatoes (350 g / 12 oz), peeled and chopped
- 2 tablespoons olive oil
- 1.5 liters (6.3 cups / 50 fl oz) vegetable broth
- 1 tablespoon white vinegar
- 1 teaspoon caraway seeds (optional)
- 30 g (1 oz) fresh parsley, chopped
- 1 pinch sugar
- 5 juniper berries, crushed
- 2 bay leaves
- 4 smoked sausages (such as Mettenden, Frankfurter, or another smoked/preboiled variety)
- Salt and black pepper to taste

Instructions

1. Peel the onions and garlic and chop them finely. Peel the potatoes and carrots and chop them into bite-sized pieces. Finely chop the parsley. Wash the cabbage, remove the outer leaves, then quarter it through the stem. Remove the dense core with a sharp knife and discard. Roughly slice the cabbage into bite-sized pieces.
2. Heat 2 tablespoons of olive oil in a large pot over medium heat. Add the onions and sauté until translucent, about 3–4 minutes. Stir in the garlic and cook for 1 more minute until fragrant.
3. Add the cabbage along with 1 teaspoon of salt and briefly fry it with the onions. The salt will help draw out moisture from the cabbage. Pour in the vegetable broth along with the crushed juniper berries, bay leaves, and caraway seeds. Cover the pot and let the cabbage cook for 40 minutes over medium-low heat.
4. Stir in the potatoes, carrots, and parsley. Continue cooking for another 20 minutes, or until the vegetables are tender.
5. Before serving, add the sugar and vinegar to taste. The exact amount depends on your preference—adjust until you reach the desired balance of sweet and sour flavors. Season with salt and black pepper to taste.
6. Add the smoked sausages to the soup. The soup no longer needs to cook—just let the sausages warm up in the hot broth for a few minutes before serving.
7. Serve hot with crusty bread or rye bread for a hearty meal.

SERVING: 6 PEOPLE **PREP:** 20 MINS **COOK:** 1 HR

Kürbissuppe

Pumpkin Soup

A delicious creamy autumn soup made with pumpkin, and potatoes. We often eat it as a main course with a slice of bread. Hokkaido is the most common pumpkin in Germany but you can use other pumpkins for this soup.

Ingredients

- 900 g (2 lb) Hokkaido pumpkin (Kuri squash) (no need to peel if using Hokkaido; other varieties may need peeling after roasting)
- 1 onion (150 g / 5 oz), finely chopped
- 2 cloves garlic, minced
- 4 carrots (300 g / 10 oz), peeled and chopped
- 2 potatoes (300 g / 10 oz), peeled and chopped
- 2 tablespoons vegetable oil
- 1.5 liters (6 cups) vegetable stock
- ½ teaspoon honey
- 100 ml (½ cup/3.3 oz) heavy cream or whipping cream
- Salt and black pepper to taste
- Pinch of nutmeg
- 15 g (½ oz) fresh parsley, finely chopped

Instructions

1. Wash the pumpkin thoroughly. If using Hokkaido (Kuri squash), there's no need to peel it. If using another variety, you may need to roast and peel it first. Cut the pumpkin in half, scoop out the seeds, and chop it into rough 3 cm (1 inch) chunks. Peel and finely dice the onion and garlic. Peel and chop the carrots and potatoes into 2 cm (¾ inch) chunks.
2. Heat 2 tablespoons of vegetable oil in a large saucepan over medium heat. Add the onion and sauté until soft, about 3–4 minutes. Stir in the garlic and cook for 1 more minute, stirring frequently.
3. Add the pumpkin, carrots, potatoes, and honey to the pot. Stir well and let them cook for about 5 minutes. Pour in the vegetable stock, ensuring all ingredients are covered.
4. Let the soup simmer over low to medium heat for about 30 minutes, or until all vegetables are soft. Use an immersion blender or a food processor to blend the soup until smooth.
5. Season with salt, black pepper, and a pinch of nutmeg, adjusting to taste. Stir in the heavy cream and freshly chopped parsley just before serving.
6. Serve warm with fresh crusty bread.

Salate

SALADS

Krautsalat

Coleslaw

This is a specialty from Bavaria. This salad, made from shredded cabbage in a sweet-and-sour vinegar marinade, pairs perfectly with Schnitzel (p. 66) or Bratwurst. It is also a popular salad to bring to a Buffet or BBQ. This salad is mayo-free, so it stays fresh for days.

Ingredients

- 900 g (2 lb) white or green cabbage
- 200 g (7 oz) white onion, finely diced
- 4 tablespoons white vinegar (use apple cider vinegar or white wine vinegar)
- 4 tablespoons vegetable oil (use a neutral oil such as sunflower or canola oil)
- 2 teaspoons salt
- 2 tablespoons sugar
- 1 teaspoon ground caraway seeds (optional, or use whole caraway seeds, or omit if preferred)
- Black pepper to taste

Instructions

1. Wash the cabbage thoroughly and remove the outer leaves. Quarter it through the stem, then use a sharp knife to remove and discard the dense core.
2. Finely shred the cabbage into thin strips using a knife, mandoline, or food processor. Transfer it to a large bowl.
3. Sprinkle 2 teaspoons of salt evenly over the cabbage. Using your hands, knead the salt into the cabbage for about 5 minutes. Let it rest for at least 20 minutes to draw out excess moisture. (This prevents the coleslaw from becoming soggy.)
4. Meanwhile, finely dice the onion.
5. Heat 2 teaspoons of oil in a frying pan over medium heat.
6. Add the onions and sauté until they turn golden brown. Remove from heat and allow to cool.
7. In a small bowl, whisk together the vinegar, remaining oil, sugar, caraway seeds, and black pepper. Stir in the cooled onions.
8. Drain the cabbage and squeeze out excess liquid. Place the drained cabbage into a salad bowl and pour the dressing over it. Mix thoroughly until combined and leave to rest for about 2 hours (ideally overnight) for the flavors to infuse.

SERVING: 4 PEOPLE **PREP:** 10 MINS **COOK:** 5 MINS

Eiersalat

Egg Salad

A signature dish of my Mum's. This sweet and refreshing egg salad is a surprisingly delightful combination of hard-boiled eggs, tart apples and crisp dill pickles. You need to try it to fully appreciate the irresistible sweet and sour taste. It is lighter on mayonnaise than other egg salad recipes but big on taste. It is perfect for sandwiches, BBQs, or savory breakfasts.

Ingredients

- 6 medium eggs
- ½ apple (tart variety, such as Granny Smith or Braeburn)
- 2–3 dill pickles (or substitute with cornichons)
- 1 teaspoon fresh lemon juice
- 3 tablespoons mayonnaise (low-fat if desired)
- 1 tablespoon chopped chives
- salt and pepper to taste

Instructions

1. Bring a small saucepan of water to a boil. Gently add the eggs and cook for about 10 minutes.
2. While the eggs are boiling, prepare the other ingredients: Peel and finely slice the apple and slice the dill pickles.
3. In a small bowl, whisk together the mayonnaise and lemon juice. Set aside.
4. Once the eggs are done, transfer them to a bowl of cold water and let them cool completely.
5. Peel the cooled eggs and finely chop them. Place them in a medium-sized bowl.
6. Add the chopped apple, sliced pickles, and chives to the bowl. Pour in the mayonnaise dressing and mix until well combined.
7. Season with salt and pepper to taste.
8. Serve the egg salad at room temperature for the best flavor. It pairs well with rye bread or a fresh baguette.

More info at https://mydinner.co.uk/german-egg-and-apple-salad/ or Google "*MyDinner Egg Salad*".

SERVING: 4 PEOPLE **PREP:** 10 MINS **REST:** 30 MINS

Gurkensalat mit Saurer Sahne

Creamy Cucumber Salad

I cannot imagine summer without this salad. This is the way my mother used to prepare her salad with sour cream, a hint of cider vinegar, and lots of freshly chopped dill. Whether you are team oil and vinegar or team creamy dressing, Gurkensalat never disappoints.

Ingredients

- 2 English cucumbers
- 2 teaspoons salt
- 180 g (¾ cup) sour cream
- 1 tablespoon olive oil
- 1 tablespoon cider vinegar
- 2 tablespoons chopped dill
- 1 teaspoon agave syrup (or substitute with sugar)
- 1 tablespoon lemon juice
- Black pepper to taste

Instructions

1. Wash the cucumbers under running water.
2. Using a mandoline slicer or a sharp knife, slice them into thin (about 2 mm) rounds.
3. Place the cucumber slices in a colander and sprinkle them with 2 teaspoons of salt. Gently mix to distribute the salt evenly and let them sit for 30 minutes to draw out excess water. Place the colander over a bowl to catch the liquid.
4. Meanwhile, prepare the dressing. In a large mixing bowl, whisk together the sour cream, lemon juice, cider vinegar, agave syrup (or sugar), and chopped dill until well combined.
5. After 30 minutes, gently squeeze out any remaining liquid from the cucumbers. Discard the excess liquid and add the cucumber slices to the dressing.
6. Mix well, then taste and adjust the seasoning with black pepper as needed. (Be mindful of the salt, as the cucumbers were pre-salted.)
7. Cover and refrigerate until ready to serve. Serve chilled for the best flavor.

More info at https://mydinner.co.uk/creamy-cucumber-salad/ or Google "*MyDinner Cucumber Salad*".

SERVING: 4 PEOPLE **PREP:** 10 MINS **REST:** 30 MINS

Gurkensalat

Cucumber Salad (Oil and Vinegar Dressing)

Gurkensalat is the lighter version of Germany's beloved cucumber salad - and my favorite, too. Paper-thin cucumber slices are tossed in a sweet-and-sour vinegar dressing with fresh dill, creating a light and refreshing side dish.

Ingredients

- 2 English cucumbers
- 1 small onion (only approx 50 gr/1.7 oz)
- 3 tablespoons white vinegar (white wine vinegar, cider vinegar or herb vinegar)
- 4 tablespoons oil (sunflower oil or rapeseed)
- 2 teaspoons sugar
- 2 tablespoons chopped dill
- 2 teaspoons salt
- pepper

Instructions

1. If you want, you can peel the cucumber. Otherwise, just clean it with a brush and then finely slice it. You can either do this by using a simple kitchen knife or a vegetable mandolin. With a mandolin, you can achieve especially thin and even slices. Place the cucumber slices in a colander and sprinkle with approximately 2 teaspoons of salt. This will draw out the excess water so you can avoid your salad from becoming soggy. Leave the cucumber to drain for around 30 minutes to an hour.
2. While the cucumbers drain, prepare the dressing by peeling and finely chopping the onion (this step is optional, but adds a nice crunch to the salad). In a jar, whisk together the vinegar, oil, chopped onion, and sugar until well combined.
3. Once the cucumbers have drained, pour the dressing over them, add the fresh dill, and toss everything together. Season with salt and pepper to taste, then serve chilled.

SERVING: 4 PEOPLE **PREP:** 10 MINS **COOK:** 5 MINS

Tomatensalat

Tomato Salad

This is time for tomatoes to shine. This simple salad is really refreshing—the honey and garlic dressing adds warmth and a little sharpness. A great everyday vitamin C boost.

Ingredients

- 500 g (1 lb) tomatoes
- 2 tablespoons olive oil
- 2 tablespoons white balsamic vinegar (or substitute with white wine vinegar for a tangier taste)
- ½ teaspoon garlic (optional)
- 1 ½ teaspoons honey (or substitute with sugar)
- ½ teaspoon salt
- ¼ teaspoon black pepper
- 3 tablespoons finely chopped spring onions/scallions (or use a regular onion)
- 3 tablespoons freshly chopped basil (or substitute with 1 teaspoon dried basil – about 10 g / 0.5 oz)
- 1 tablespoon freshly chopped parsley (or substitute with ½ teaspoon dried parsley – about 5 g / 0.17 oz)

Instructions

Dressing

1. Add the olive oil, vinegar, garlic, honey, salt, and pepper into a bowl and stir until the honey has dissolved. (You can prepare this dressing up to three days in advance.)

Salad

1. First, wash the tomatoes and remove the stems if necessary. Slice them in half, remove the core, and chop them into bite-sized pieces (about ¾-inch chunks). There is no need to deseed the tomatoes.
2. Next, remove the outer, dry leaves of the scallions/spring onions and trim off any wilted tips. Chop the spring onions into thin rings, stopping at the root base, then discard the root. Remove the parsley and basil leaves from their stems and finely chop them.
3. Place the tomatoes, spring onions, basil, and parsley in a bowl. Pour the dressing over the top and toss everything until well combined.
4. You can serve the salad immediately or let it rest in the fridge. Note: The garlic flavor will intensify the longer the salad sits.

SERVING: 4 PEOPLE **PREP:** 10 MINS

Karottensalat

Carrot Salad with Apple

My mother's signature dish – and my readers agree. Sweet, a little sour, and super refreshing. We always had it as a side for Abendbrot (evening meal), and today it's one of the salads my children eat without a murmur.

Ingredients

- 700 g (1 ½ lb, about 5 large) carrots
- 1 tart apple

For the carrot salad dressing

- 2 tablespoons sunflower oil (or any other plant-based oil)
- 2 tablespoons cider vinegar (or substitute with white wine vinegar)
- 1 tablespoon fresh lemon juice
- 1 teaspoon sugar (or substitute with honey or a sugar replacement)

To serve (optional)

- 2 tablespoons fresh herbs, such as chives or parsley
- 2 tablespoons seeds or nuts, such as sunflower or pumpkin seeds, walnuts, or hazelnuts

Instructions

1. Peel the carrots and remove the tops.
2. Peel and core the apple.
3. Using a hand grater or a food processor, shred the carrots into thin strips, ensuring they retain some texture. Repeat with the apple.
4. In a separate bowl, prepare the dressing by whisking together the sunflower oil, vinegar, lemon juice, and sugar until well combined.
5. Pour the dressing over the shredded carrots and apple, tossing gently to coat.
6. Season with salt and pepper to taste.
7. Let the salad marinate for at least an hour to allow the flavors to blend.
8. Before serving, garnish with fresh herbs such as parsley or chives (optional). For added texture and flavor, sprinkle with nuts, seeds, or raisins.
9. Serve chilled and enjoy!

SERVING: 4 PEOPLE **PREP:** 10 MINS **COOK:** 20 MINS **REST:** 2 HRS

Norddeutscher Kartoffelsalat

North German Potato Salad

In Northern Germany, a potato salad with a creamy dressing is traditional. I like this dressing in particular because it's not as heavy as pure mayo dressings. Add the eggs if desired, but the salad also tastes great without them.

Ingredients

- 900 g (2 lb) waxy potatoes
- 3 medium eggs, hard-boiled (optional)
- 120 g (4 oz) white onion
- 1 tablespoon neutral oil
- 100 g (3 ½ oz) pickled gherkins
- 1 tablespoon white vinegar
- 1 teaspoon white sugar
- 2 teaspoons mustard (preferably German mustard, but Dijon will work)
- 180 ml (6 fl oz, ¾ cup) vegetable stock/broth
- 6 tablespoons mayonnaise
- 3 tablespoons yogurt
- 20 g (1 oz) fresh dill

Instructions

1. Place the potatoes in a pot of salted water and bring to a boil. Cook until soft, about 20 minutes.
2. Meanwhile, hard-boil the eggs (8–10 minutes). Let them cool completely before using.
3. Peel and finely chop the onion. In a pan over low heat, sauté the onion in the oil for about 10 minutes until soft and translucent.
4. Stir in the mustard and vinegar with the broth until combined.
5. Dice the pickled gherkins. Peel the eggs and cut them into small cubes.
6. Once the potatoes are cooked, peel them and slice them into bite-sized pieces. While the potatoes are still warm, place them in a large salad bowl and pour over the warm broth mixture. Stir gently and season with salt and pepper to taste.
7. Add the gherkins and eggs, then let the salad rest for about 2 hours—either in the fridge or at room temperature.
8. Before serving, mix in the mayonnaise and yogurt. Lastly, chop the dill and stir it into the salad.

More info at https://mydinner.co.uk/northern-german-potato-salad/ or Google "*MyDinner North German Potato Salad*".

SERVING: 6 PEOPLE **PREP:** 10 MINS **COOK:** 20 MINS

Schwäbischer Kartoffelsalat

Swabian Potato Salad

The famous Swabian. In Swabia, they say the texture should be "schlotzig." This means it should be shiny and moist. You want to hear a "squelching" sound when you poke your fork into it.

Ingredients

- 1 kg (35 oz) waxy potatoes
- 200 g (7 oz) onions
- 3 tablespoons vegetable oil (e.g., rapeseed oil or sunflower oil)
- 2 ½ tablespoons white vinegar (e.g., herb or white wine vinegar)
- 200 ml (6.7 fl oz, ¾ cup + 1 tablespoon) stock/broth (For an authentic Swabian version, use beef broth; for a vegetarian option, use vegetable broth.)
- 3 teaspoons of mustard (Use German mustard or substitute with Dijon mustard).
- ½ teaspoon salt
- ¼ teaspoon sugar
- 30 g (1 oz) chives (Can be replaced with spring onions or parsley.)

Instructions

1. Wash the potatoes thoroughly and boil them in salted water until tender but not overcooked.
2. Meanwhile, peel and finely chop the onions.
3. Prepare the vinaigrette by heating the broth and whisking in the vinegar, oil, and mustard until well combined. Add the chopped onions to the hot vinaigrette—this helps to mellow their sharpness.
4. Season the vinaigrette with sugar and salt to taste. (Be mindful of the salt level, as different broths may vary in saltiness.)
5. Once the potatoes are cooked, drain and peel them while still warm. Then, finely slice them into thin rounds.
6. Gradually pour the warm vinaigrette over the warm potatoes, stirring gently after each addition. In Swabian cuisine, the perfect consistency is "schlotzig"—a soft, slightly creamy, and moist texture. The exact amount of vinaigrette needed may vary depending on the variety of potatoes used.
7. Let the salad rest for at least one hour to allow the flavors to develop and the dressing to absorb. For the best results, let it sit overnight.
8. Just before serving, sprinkle with freshly chopped chives or other herbs such as parsley or finely sliced spring onions. Adjust the seasoning with salt and pepper if needed.
9. Serve at room temperature for the most authentic flavor.

More info at https://mydinner.co.uk/swabian-potato-salad/ or Google "*MyDinner Swabian Potato Salad*" .

SERVING: 4 PEOPLE **PREP:** 10 MINS **COOK:** 20 MINS

Kartoffelsalat mit Speck

Potato Salad with Bacon

This Bavarian potato salad has a thick roux dressing that gently coats the potatoes. This traditional southern German recipe features crispy bacon, gently fried onions, and tangy pickles. You can serve it cool or warm.

Ingredients

- 1 kg (2 lb) waxy potatoes (such as Yukon Gold, red potatoes, Charlotte, or new potatoes)
- 1 teaspoon salt
- 150 g (5 oz) bacon (Speck is preferred, but streaky bacon works well)
- 1 onion (150 g / 5 oz), finely chopped (white or red onion)
- 100 g (3.5 oz / ½ cup) pickled gherkins, chopped
- 2 tablespoons neutral oil (such as sunflower oil, canola oil, or vegetable oil)
- 240 ml (1 cup) hot beef broth
- 1 tablespoon all-purpose flour
- 1 teaspoon sugar
- 4 tablespoons white wine vinegar (can be replaced with cider vinegar)
- 4 tablespoons fresh herbs (such as chopped chives and parsley)
- Salt and black pepper to taste

Instructions

1. Thoroughly wash the potatoes and place them, unpeeled, in a large pot of water. Add 1 teaspoon of salt and bring to a boil. Cook until fork-tender, about 15–20 minutes.
2. While the potatoes are cooking, finely chop the onion and gherkins. If necessary, cube the bacon.
3. Heat 2 tablespoons of oil in a frying pan over medium heat. Add the bacon and cook until crispy. Then, add the onions and sauté until soft and translucent, about 3 minutes.
4. Sprinkle 1 tablespoon of flour over the bacon-onion mixture and stir constantly for about 1 minute. Gradually pour in the hot beef stock, stirring constantly, until the dressing thickens slightly. Stir in the sugar, vinegar, and chopped gherkins.
5. Drain the cooked potatoes and peel them while still warm. Then slice them into bite-sized pieces and place them in a large bowl. Pour the hot dressing over the warm potatoes and toss gently to combine.
6. Let the salad sit for 20 minutes to absorb the flavors.
7. Just before serving, stir in the fresh herbs and season with salt and pepper to taste. Serve warm.

More info at https://mydinner.co.uk/potato-salad-with-bacon/ or Google "*MyDinner Potato Salad with Bacon*".

SERVING: 4 PEOPLE **PREP:** 10 MINS **COOK:** 15 MINS

Nudelsalat

Pasta Salad

I bring this pasta salad to every BBQ. It's quick to prepare and super popular with the kids. It tastes even better the next day, once the pasta has absorbed all the flavors. You can make it either with Frankfurter sausages or Fleischwurst (Bologna).

Ingredients

- 250 g (9 oz / ½ lb / 2 cups) pasta (fusillini, rotini, or similar)
- 200 g (7 oz) sausage (Frankfurter, Bockwurst, Bologna, or any smoked sausage)
- 250 g (9 oz / ¾ cup) mayonnaise
- 1 can (400 g/ 1lb) peas and carrots, drained
- 1 teaspoon mustard (German mustard or Dijon Mustard)
- 100 g (about 3.5 oz / 3 large gherkins) pickled gherkins
- 1 tablespoon vinegar (from the pickled gherkin jar)
- 2 tablespoons fresh herbs (such as chives, parsley, or dill; optional)
- Salt and pepper to taste

Instructions

1. Cook the pasta according to the package instructions until al dente. Drain and set aside to cool slightly (it can still be slightly warm when mixing).
2. Slice the sausages into ½-inch (1–2 cm) pieces.
3. Finely chop the gherkins.
4. Drain the liquid from the canned peas and carrots, then rinse.
5. In a small bowl, whisk together the mayonnaise, mustard, and gherkin brine until smooth.
6. Once the pasta has cooled, transfer it to a large mixing bowl. Add the chopped gherkins, drained vegetables, and sliced sausages.
7. Pour the dressing over the pasta mixture and stir until everything is well combined.
8. If using fresh herbs, mix them in now.
9. Season the salad with salt and pepper and adjust to taste.
10. For the best flavor, let the salad rest for at least 20 minutes to allow the pasta to absorb the dressing. For optimal results, refrigerate overnight before serving.

More info at https://mydinner.co.uk/german-cold-pasta-salad/ or Google "*MyDinner* German Pasta Salad" .

Beilagen
SIDE DISHES

SERVING: 4 PEOPLE **PREP:** 20 MINS **COOK:** 20 MINS

Kartoffelpuffer

Potato Pancakes

These crispy golden Kartoffelpuffer (also known as Reibekuchen) are a staple dish in my kitchen—my kids beg for them weekly! There's something so satisfying about watching their faces light up when I serve these perfectly crunchy potato pancakes. Whether topped with applesauce (p. 50) for the little ones or sour cream for grown-ups, they disappear instantly.

Ingredients

- 900 g (2 lb) waxy potatoes waxy, (i.e. Yukon Gold or Charlotte potatoes)
- 1 onion (120 g/ 4 oz)
- 2 medium eggs
- 3 tablespoons all-purpose flour
- 1 pinch nutmeg, optional
- 1 teaspoon salt

Instructions

1. Peel and finely grate the potatoes and onion. Place in a kitchen towel and squeeze out all the starchy water into a bowl. Transfer the squeezed mixture to a separate bowl. Pour away the potato water, but keep the starchy remains at the bottom and add them to the potatoes.
2. Add the eggs, salt, flour and nutmeg (if using) and mix until combined.
3. Add generous oil or clarified butter to a large frying pan to cover the bottom. Once heated, spoon potato mixture into the pan (about 15 cm diameter). Press flat with a fork - don't make them too thick.
4. Fry at medium heat for 5 minutes per side until golden. Test the first one to ensure it's cooked through.
5. Place Kartoffelpuffer on a kitchen towel-lined plate to absorb excess oil. Keep warm in a low oven (100°C/200°F) while frying remaining pancakes.
6. Serve with cinnamon and sugar, homemade Apfelmus, or sour cream.

Find more images and tips at https://mydinner.co.uk/kartoffelpuffer/ or Google *"MyDinner Kartoffelpuffer"*.

SERVING: 4 PEOPLE **PREP:** 30 MINS **COOK:** 20 MINS

Kartoffelklöße

Potato Dumplings

I always thought potato dumplings were complicated to make—until I learned this recipe. Made from mashed potatoes and starch, it this recipe helps you prepare them in no time. Plus, the taste doesn't even compare to store-bought.

Ingredients

- 1 kg (2 lb) starchy potatoes (such as Maris Piper or Yukon Gold)
- 200 g (7 oz or about 1 ½ cups) potato starch or cornstarch
- 2 egg yolks
- 2 tablespoons butter (plus 2 tablespoons more for serving)
- ¼ teaspoon grated nutmeg
- 3 teaspoons salt or more to taste
- 2 tablespoons chopped fresh parsley (for serving)

Instructions

1. Peel potatoes and place in a large pot with 1 teaspoon salt and enough water to cover them. Bring to a boil.
2. Boil for about 20 minutes until fork-tender, depending on potato size.
3. Drain, then return to the pot over low heat briefly to evaporate remaining moisture.
4. Mash potatoes with a ricer or masher until smooth.
5. Transfer to a large bowl and mix in 2 tablespoons butter, potato starch (or cornstarch), egg yolks, 1 teaspoon salt, and ¼ teaspoon nutmeg.
6. Mix until just combined—avoid overmixing to prevent dense, tough dough.
7. Bring a large pot of salted water (1 teaspoon salt) to a boil, then reduce to a gentle simmer to prevent dumplings from breaking apart.
8. Gently lower dumplings into simmering water and cook 15–20 minutes until they float. Remove with a slotted spoon.

Parsley Butter

1. Melt 2 tablespoons of butter in a small saucepan over low heat.
2. Stir in chopped parsley and drizzle over dumplings before serving.

SERVING: 4 PEOPLE **PREP:** 30 MINS **COOK:** 20 MINS

Semmelknödel

Bread Dumplings

Perfect for leftover rolls or baguette. These dumplings soak up gravy beautifully. Experiment with the milk-to-bread ratio since it depends on how dry your bread is—always cook a test dumpling first so you can adjust the texture as needed.

Ingredients

- 4 crusty rolls (250 g / 9 oz can be substituted with a baguette)
- 2 medium eggs at room temperature
- 180 ml (⅓ cups) milk (full-fat)
- 1 large onion (about 150 g/5 oz)
- 2 tablespoons chopped parsley
- 2 tablespoons butter
- 1 teaspoon salt
- ¼ teaspoon pepper
- 50 g (½ cup) bacon cubed
- Optional: more milk and breadcrumbs.

Instructions

1. Chop the rolls into small cubes, about 1 cm (½ inch) in size.
2. In a saucepan or microwave, warm the milk until hot but not boiling. Season with 1 teaspoon of salt and pour over the bread cubes. Let sit while preparing the other ingredients.
3. Peel and finely chop the onion. If using, cube the bacon. In a frying pan, melt the butter over medium-low heat. Add the onion (and bacon, if using) and sauté until the onions are translucent, about 5-7 minutes.
4. Add the cooked onion, bacon, and chopped parsley to the soaked bread cubes. Mix thoroughly with a spoon and let the mixture rest for 10-15 minutes to allow the flavors to meld.
5. In the meantime, bring a large pot (at least 5 liters) of water to a boil. Add 1 teaspoon of salt. Once boiling, reduce the heat to maintain a gentle simmer.
6. Beat the eggs and add to the bread mixture. Season with additional salt and pepper to taste. Mix thoroughly.

More info at https://mydinner.co.uk/semmelknodel/ or Google "*MyDinner Bread Dumpling*".

Semmelknödel

Bread Dumplings

7. Knead the mixture with clean hands (or use gloves if preferred). If the dough feels too soft or sticky, ad breadcrumbs a little at a time until it firms up. If the dough is too dry or crumbly, add a small amount of milk until it reaches a pliable consistency.
8. With wet hands, shape the dough into 8-10 evenly sized balls, depending on your preferred size. For uniform dumplings, use an ice cream scoop to portion the dough. Press gently but firmly to make it compact and smooth, ensuring there are no cracks or bulges that could cause them to fall apart during cooking.
9. Carefully lower the dumplings into the simmering water. Do not boil, as this can cause them to lose shape. Simmer gently for about 20 minutes, or until the dumplings float to the surface.
10. Remove the dumplings with a slotted spoon and serve warm. They pair perfectly with Jäger sauce a as side for schnitzel.

SERVING: 4 PEOPLE **PREP:** 30 MINS **COOK:** 1 HR

Apfelrotkohl

Red Cabbage with Apple

Back when I was living in England, I missed this dish so much it actually prompted me to start learning how to make German recipes from scratch. Red cabbage is a popular side dish for Sauerbraten (p. 60), Goulash (p. 53), and game. For me this dish represents Germany, and I have put my own twist on it.

Ingredients

- 1 kg (2 lbs) red cabbage
- 2 onions (approx. 150 g / 5 oz), peeled and finely sliced
- 3 tart/sour apples (approx. 400 g / 14 oz), peeled, cored, and cubed (see notes for best varieties)
- 50 g (2 tablespoons) butter (or 2 tablespoons vegetable oil for a vegan option)
- 1 bay leaf
- 4 whole cloves
- 1 cinnamon stick
- 60 ml (2 fl oz/ ¼ cup) red wine vinegar - can be substituted with apple cider vinegar
- 120 ml (4 fl oz/ ½ cup) water
- 2 tablespoon sugar
- 1 teaspoon salt
- (Optional) 1 tablespoon flour + 2 tablespoon water (to thicken if needed)

Instructions

Stovetop Method

1. Remove the outer leaves and tough stalk from the red cabbage. Wash and cut into thin strips. For convenience, use a food processor to shred it. Transfer to a bowl and pour the red wine vinegar over it.
2. Peel and finely slice the onions.
3. Peel, core, and cut the apples into approximately 3 cm (1.2-inch) cubes.
4. In a large saucepan, melt the butter (or heat the oil) over medium heat. Add the onions and sauté until they begin to brown.
5. Add the sugar and apples, cooking until they start to slightly caramelize.
6. Stir in the red cabbage and cook for 5 minutes, stirring frequently to prevent burning.
7. Add the bay leaf, cloves, salt, cinnamon stick, and water. Cover with a lid and let it simmer on low heat for about 1 hour, stirring occasionally to prevent sticking.
8. If the cabbage is too watery mix 1 tablespoon of flour with 2 tablespoons of water in a small bowl and stir it into the pot.

More info at https://mydinner.co.uk/german-red-cabbage-and-apple/ or Google "*MyDinner Red Cabbage*".

Apfelrotkohl

Red Cabbage with Apple

9. Adjust the seasoning with more sugar or salt to taste.
10. Serve immediately, or refrigerate and serve the next day for enhanced flavor. This dish also freezes well.

Slow Cooker Method

1. Grease the bowl of your slow cooker with butter or oil.
2. Remove the outer leaves and stalk from the red cabbage, wash, and cut into thin strips. Using a food processor can save time. Transfer to a bowl and pour the red wine vinegar over it.
3. Peel and cube the onions.
4. Peel, core, and chop the apples into approximately 2 cm (0.8-inch) cubes.
5. Add all ingredients to the slow cooker.
6. Cover and cook on low for about 5 hours.
7. Stir occasionally and adjust the seasoning before serving

More info at https://mydinner.co.uk/german-red-cabbage-and-apple/ or Google "*MyDinner Red Cabbage*".

SERVING: 4 PEOPLE **PREP:** 10 MINS **COOK:** 25 MINS

Bratkartoffeln

Fried Potatoes

Fried potatoes with onions and bacon are one of my true comfort foods. You can serve it them as a side dish, but my family often eats as a main meal with a fried egg on top. This recipe yields enough for a side dish. If serving as a main dish, scale up the ingredient amounts accordingly.

Ingredients

- 1 onion (about 100 g / 3.5 oz) diced
- 150 g (5 oz) smoked bacon (breakfast bacon or bacon lardons can be used), cubed
- 600 g (21 oz) boiled potatoes (best if boiled the day before), sliced about ½ cm (¼ inch) thick
- 3 tablespoons clarified butter (or use sunflower oil plus 1 teaspoon butter)
- Salt and Pepper to taste
- 1 handful (about 15 g / ½ oz) fresh parsley, finely chopped

Instructions

1. Cube the onion and bacon.
2. Heat 1 tablespoon clarified butter in a frying pan over medium heat. Add bacon and fry until slightly crispy, then add onion and cook until translucent. (Don't burn the onion—it creates bitterness.)
3. Remove bacon and onion from pan and set aside.
4. Peel the boiled potatoes, then slice into 0.5 cm (¼ inch) thick slices.
5. Melt remaining 2 tablespoons clarified butter in the same pan. Add potato slices and fry over medium heat until crispy. Let each side cook undisturbed for 3–4 minutes before turning. Ensure potatoes have enough space for even frying. If the pan is too small, fry in batches rather than overcrowding. Don't stir —flip individually with a spatula to maintain crisp texture.
6. After about 20 minutes, return onions and bacon to the pan. Fry together for another 2 minutes, carefully turning potatoes.
7. Season with salt and pepper.
8. Before serving, sprinkle with chopped parsley for freshness.

More info at https://mydinner.co.uk/bratkartoffeln-recipe-german-home-fries/ or Google "*MyDinner Bratkartoffeln*

SERVING: 6 PEOPLE **PREP:** 20 MINS **COOK:** 20 MINS

Spätzle

Egg Dumplings

Spätzle – the soft, buttery dumplings – are pretty high on my list of favorite foods. They're quite quick to make, but to my husband's dismay, I somehow manage to get the dough everywhere. Check out the website if you have yet to purchase a spätzle maker. A must-try recipe in this cookbook.

Ingredients

- 6 medium eggs, at room temperature
- 180 ml (7 fl oz or ¾ cup) milk
- 1 tablespoon unsalted butter, melted
- 1 teaspoon salt
- 500 g (17 oz or 4 cups) all-purpose flour
- 1 tablespoon butter (optional, for reheating the Spaetzle)

Instructions

1. In a large mixing bowl, whisk together the eggs, salt, milk, and melted butter.
2. Sift the flour over the top, then immediately mix everything into a loose, elastic dough using a wooden spoon, hand mixer, or stand mixer. Continue mixing until the dough becomes smooth and bubbly.
3. Let the dough rest for about 10 minutes to allow the gluten to develop.
4. Meanwhile, bring a large pot of water to a boil and add a pinch of salt.
5. Using your chosen Spaetzle maker, press the dough through, allowing the strands to drop directly into the boiling water.
6. The Spaetzle will float to the top once they are cooked. Remove them with a slotted spoon. (Be careful not to cook too many at once, as this may cause them to stick)
7. If serving immediately, plate the freshly cooked Spaetzle straight from the water.
8. For make-ahead preparation, transfer the cooked Spaetzle to a bowl of ice water to stop further cooking.
9. When ready to serve, heat a frying pan with browned butter and reheat the Spätzle in it—this is the traditional method used in German restaurants for locking in extra flavor.

More info at https://mydinner.co.uk/ridiculously-easy-german-spatzle-recipe/ or Google '*MyDinner Spaetzle Recipe*'.

SERVING: 12 PEOPLE **PREP:** 10 MINS **COOK:** 35 MINS **REST:** 45 MINS

Zwiebelkuchen

Onion Pie

This savory onion pie is made for warm late summer evenings. Perfect to share with friends, accompanied by a young white wine such as Federweisser. You can take a shortcut by using a shop-bought short crust or pizza dough for the base.

Ingredients

For the Yeast Dough:

- 180 ml (6 fl oz / ¾ cup) lukewarm milk
- ½ teaspoon sugar
- 7 g (2 teaspoons) instant yeast (1 pouch)
- 1 teaspoon salt
- 310 g (11 oz / 1 ¾ cups + 2 tablespoons) all-purpose flour (Germany: Type 405, UK: Plain flour)
- 2 tablespoons vegetable oil

For the Onion Filling:

- 1 kg (2 lb / 35 oz) onions, thinly sliced
- 200 g (7 oz) smoked bacon, cubed
- 1 tablespoon vegetable oil
- ¼ teaspoon ground caraway seeds (optional)
- 400 g (14 oz / 1 ¾ cups) sour cream
- 3 medium eggs
- Salt and pepper to taste

- **To Garnish (Optional):**
- 4 tablespoons chopped chives

Instructions

Preparing the Dough

1. In a small bowl, combine the instant yeast and sugar with the lukewarm milk. Stir gently and let it rest for 10 minutes until the yeast activates and small bubbles begin to form on the surface.
2. In a large mixing bowl, whisk together the flour and salt. Pour in the yeast-milk mixture and vegetable oil.
3. Using a stand mixer or hand mixer with a dough hook attachment, knead the dough for about 5 minutes until it becomes smooth and elastic, and pulls away from the sides of the bowl.
4. Lightly grease a large bowl with oil or nonstick spray. Place the dough in the bowl, turning it to coat all sides lightly with oil.
5. Cover the bowl with plastic wrap, aluminum foil, or a clean kitchen towel. Let the dough rise in a warm place for 45 minutes, or until it has doubled in size.

Zwiebelkuchen
Onion Pie

Preparing the Onion Topping

- While the dough is rising, prepare the onion mixture.
- Peel the onions and slice them into thin rings. Cut the bacon into small pieces.
- Heat 1 tablespoon of vegetable oil in a frying pan over medium heat. Add the bacon and fry until crispy.
- Add the onions to the pan and sauté over low to medium heat until they become soft and translucent. This should take about 10 minutes—slow cooking allows the onions to develop their natural sweetness.
- Remove the onion mixture from the heat and let it cool slightly.
- In a separate bowl, whisk together the sour cream and eggs. Add this mixture to the cooled onions and bacon, then stir in the caraway seeds. Season with salt and pepper to taste

Assembling and Baking

1. Preheat the oven to 200°C (392°F). Grease a baking tray (mine was 30 cm x 40 xm , 12" x 16') with butter or line it with parchment paper.
2. Once the dough has risen, transfer it to a floured surface and knead it briefly by hand. Roll it out into a thin rectangle.
3. Lift the dough into the prepared baking tray and press it into the corners, creating a small rim around the edges.
4. Pour the onion-bacon mixture evenly over the dough.
5. Bake in the preheated oven for 35 minutes, or until the crust is golden brown and the filling is set.
6. Allow the Zwiebelkuchen to cool slightly before serving. Garnish with freshly chopped chives, if desired.

More info at https://mydinner.co.uk/a-german-cake-with-onions/ or Google "*MyDinner Onion Cake*" .

SERVING: 4 PEOPLE **PREP:** 5 MINS **COOK:** 15 MINS

Speckbohnen

Green Beans with Bacon

This humble green bean side dish is so easy to make, yet it deserves all the fame and glory because it is simply delicious. I like to serve it with Frikadellen (p. 72) or meatloaf (p. 71).

Ingredients

- 300 g (11 oz) green beans
- 1 onion (100 g / 3.5 oz) finely chopped
- 1 tablespoon butter
- 60 g (2 oz) speck, bacon, or pancetta, diced
- 190 ml (6.5 fl oz / about ¾ cup) vegetable broth or stock
- ½ teaspoon summer savory (optional)
- Salt and pepper to taste

Instructions

1. Wash the green beans thoroughly. Trim off the tips with a sharp knife and discard them. If using runner beans, remove the tough string along the side. Then, chop the beans diagonally into 1–2 cm (½–¾ inch) wide pieces.
2. Peel and finely chop the onion into small cubes.
3. In a large skillet, melt the butter over medium heat. Add the chopped onion and sauté until soft and translucent.
4. Add the speck (or bacon/pancetta) to the pan and fry until it begins to crisp up.
5. Place the chopped beans into the skillet and pour in just enough vegetable broth or stock to cover the bottom of the pan.
6. Cover with a lid and steam the beans over low to medium heat for 10–15 minutes, or until tender. (Check occasionally—if the liquid evaporates too quickly and the beans are not yet fully cooked, add a splash more broth as needed.)
7. Before serving, season the beans with salt, black pepper, and summer savory (Bohnenkraut), if using.

More info at https://mydinner.co.uk/speckbohnen/ or Google "*MyDinner Speckbohnen*".

SERVING: 4 PEOPLE **PREP:** 5 MINS **COOK:** 15 MINS

Sauerkraut

Braised Fermented Cabbage

This is the most popular way to eat sauerkraut in Germany. By cooking it, it transforms the sauerkraut into a mellow and comforting side dish. We usually serve it as a side with bratwurst and pork. It also tastes great as a sauce for boiled potatoes, Schupfnudeln *(p. 44)* *or Spätzle.* *(p. 38)*

Ingredients

- 750 g (1½ lb) sauerkraut (1 jar)
- 1 tablespoon neutral oil (such as rapeseed or sunflower oil)
- 1 onion (100 g / 3.5 oz), finely diced
- 75 g (2.6 oz / ½ cup) bacon or speck, cubed
- 1 teaspoon sugar
- 5 juniper berries
- 2 bay leaves
- 10 peppercorns
- 1 teaspoon caraway seeds (optional)
- 240 ml (1 cup) beef broth
- 120 ml (½ cup) apple juice (optional)

Instructions

1. Drain the sauerkraut by removing it from the jar and letting the excess liquid drain off. If desired, gently squeeze out any excess moisture.
2. Finely dice the onion and bacon.
3. In a large saucepan, heat the oil over medium heat. Add the onions and sauté until soft and translucent.
4. Add the bacon cubes and sprinkle them with sugar. Fry for a few more minutes, allowing the sugar to caramelize the bacon and onions, enhancing their flavor.
5. Stir in the spices: juniper berries, peppercorns, bay leaves, and caraway seeds (if using).
6. Add the drained sauerkraut to the saucepan and stir well to combine.
7. Pour in the beef broth and, if using, the apple juice. Stir everything.
8. Reduce the heat to low, cover, and let the sauerkraut simmer gently for about 40 minutes, stirring occasionally.
9. Remove the bay leaves and juniper berries before serving. Serve warm as a side dish to sausages, pork, or other traditional German dishes.

SERVING: 4 PEOPLE **PREP:** 5 MINS **COOK:** 15 MINS

Rahmwirsing

Creamed Savoy Cabbage

This recipe is a real gem – hearty, simple, and very versatile. It might sound rich, but there isn't actually that much cream in it. We usually enjoy it with mashed potatoes, but it also makes a great pasta sauce.

Ingredients

- 500 g (17 oz) savoy cabbage (about ½ a small head)
- 1 onion (100 g / 3.5 oz), finely chopped
- 100 g (3.5 oz) bacon, cubed (optional)
- 50 g (1.7 oz / 3.5 tablespoon) butter (for a vegan version, use vegetable margarine)
- 50 g (1.7 oz / 6 tablespoon) all-purpose flour
- 480 ml (16 fl oz / approx. 2 cups) vegetable stock or broth
- 60 ml (2oz / ¼ cup) heavy cream (or more if you prefer extra creaminess)

Seasoning

- Freshly grated nutmeg, to taste
- ½ teaspoon cayenne pepper (optional, for a little spice)
- Salt, to taste
- Black pepper to taste

Instructions

1. Bring a large pot of salted water to boil.
2. While waiting for water to boil, remove dark outer cabbage leaves. Quarter the cabbage and remove the hard stem by cutting along the core. Place quartered cabbage on its flat side and finely slice into strips (about 5 mm wide). Alternatively, use a mandoline or food processor.
3. Blanch cabbage in boiling water for 4–7 minutes over medium heat. Leaves should soften but maintain their bold color.
4. Drain cabbage and cool in ice water to stop cooking and retain green color. If no ice available, place in cold water, drain immediately, and replace with more cold water until cooled. (If you don't have broth, save the cabbage water.)
5. In a saucepan, melt butter over medium heat. Add diced onion and bacon (if using) and sauté until onion turns soft and translucent.
6. Add flour and stir with wooden spoon until it forms a thick, smooth paste.
7. Slowly pour in hot broth (or reserved cabbage water), stirring continuously to prevent lumps.
8. Add cream, bring to a boil, then reduce heat to simmer.

More info at https://mydinner.co.uk/creamed-cabbage/ or Google "*MyDinner Creamed Cabbage*" .

SERVING: 4 PEOPLE **PREP:** 5 MINS **COOK:** 15 MINS

Schupfnudeln

Potato Noodles

For me, Schupfnudeln are a delicious comfort food! Here you can buy them ready-made, but I soon learned that rolling these yourself by hand is doubly satisfying. These golden, finger-shaped beauties are crispy on the outside, pillowy soft within. They're like German gnocchi's rustic cousin, perfect with sauerkraut (*p. 42**) or Jäger sauce (**p. 47**)*

Ingredients

- 500 g (1 lb 2 oz) potatoes - floury/starchy potatoes such as Russet Potatoes, Maris Piper or Yukon Gold
- 120 g (1 cup) flour
- 2 tablespoons cornstarch (cornflour in UK English)
- 1 medium egg
- 1 teaspoon salt
- ¼ teaspoon ground nutmeg (optional)
- Salt for the cooking water

For frying

- 2 tablespoons butter or neutral oil

To serve

- 1 tablespoon chopped parsley

Instructions

1. Place potatoes in a saucepan, cover with water, add 1 teaspoon salt and bring to a boil. Cook 15-20 minutes until soft.
2. Drain and let steam off so potatoes are dry before peeling.
3. Mash the potatoes using a potato masher, fork, or ricer (ricer works best to avoid lumps).
4. In a large bowl, combine mashed potatoes with flour, corn starch, egg, salt and nutmeg. Knead to a homogeneous dough, adding more flour if too sticky.
5. On a well-floured surface, roll dough into 2.5 cm thick rolls, then cut into 2.5 cm slices. Roll each slice into noodles with tapered ends for the traditional Schupfnudeln shape. Store on a floured board.
6. Heat a large pot of water with 1 teaspoon salt until simmering (not wildly bubbling). Add noodles with a slotted spoon. They're ready when they float to the top.
7. Cover with olive oil if frying later to prevent sticking.
8. To serve, fry in oil and butter until browned on all sides. Garnish with fresh parsley.

Soßen

SAUCES AND GRAVIES

SERVING: 4 PEOPLE **PREP:** 5 MINS **COOK:** 15 MINS

Jägersoße
Mushroom Sauce

One of the most popular recipes on my website! This rich mushroom sauce is perfect as a vegetarian dish served with Spätzle (p. 38) or Semmelknödel (p. 33). You can also serve it with Schnitzel (p. 66), which turns it into a classic Jägerschnitzel.

Ingredients

- 400 g (14 oz) mushrooms (I used champignons – white button mushrooms, but any variety works.)
- 150 ml (5 fl oz / ⅔ cup) whipping cream (at least 30% fat)
- 150 ml (5 fl oz / ⅔ cup) beef broth (beef broth has a stronger flavor and enhances the brown color of the sauce. Alternatively, use vegetable broth for a vegetarian version.)
- 1 onion (60 g / 2 oz), finely chopped
- 2 tablespoons butter (or oil)
- 1 tablespoon tomato paste
- 1 teaspoon balsamic vinegar
- 1 teaspoon dried thyme (or fresh thyme, if available)
- 2 tablespoon fresh parsley, finely chopped
- Salt and black pepper to taste
- 2 tablespoons cornstarch

Instructions

1. Clean mushrooms with a damp paper towel or brush and slice into 0.5 cm (¼ inch) pieces.
2. Peel and finely chop the onion. Finely chop the parsley.
3. In a large skillet, heat 1 tablespoon butter (or oil) over medium heat. Add mushrooms and sauté until they start to brown. (Mushrooms release moisture quickly, so remove before they shrink too much.) Set aside.
4. In the same pan, heat the remaining 1 tablespoon butter (or oil/lard). Add onions and sauté until they begin to brown.
5. Stir in tomato paste and cook for another minute, allowing it to slightly caramelize—this enhances flavor depth and gives the sauce a rich brown color.
6. Deglaze the pan by pouring in broth and cream, stirring well to combine.
7. Return mushrooms to the pan and season with salt and black pepper.
8. Stir in thyme, parsley, and balsamic vinegar, then let the sauce simmer until it thickens to the desired consistency.
9. To thicken the sauce, mix cornstarch with 2 tablespoons of water to form a smooth paste. Stir into the sauce and bring back to a boil.
10. If the sauce becomes too thick, adjust by adding more broth.

More info at https://mydinner.co.uk/jager-sauce/or Google *"MyDinner Jager Sauce"*.

SERVING: 4 PEOPLE **PREP:** 2 MINS **COOK:** 10 MINS

Rahmsauce

Cream Sauce

A simple cream sauce that goes well with Meatloaf (p.71) and Frikadellen (p.72). It is my go-to recipe when I am short on time, but my family is demanding a gravy with their meal.

Ingredients

- 50 gr (3 ½ tablespoons) butter
- 50 gr (3 tablespoons) all-purpose flour
- 400 ml (14 fl oz / 1 ⅔ cups) beef broth or stock (you can also use vegetable or chicken broth, but beef broth gives the sauce its rich brown color)
- 1 tablespoon tomato paste
- 90 ml (3 fl oz / ⅓ cup) whipping cream (at least 30% fat)
- salt and pepper to taste

For serving (optional):

- 2 tablespoons fresh parsley, finely chopped

Instructions

1. In a saucepan, melt the butter over medium heat.
2. Add the flour, stirring continuously with a whisk until it forms a smooth, thick paste (also called roux).
3. Gradually pour in the hot broth, whisking constantly to prevent lumps.
4. Bring the sauce to a boil, then reduce the heat to a simmer. Let it cook for 9–10 minutes, allowing the floury taste to disappear and the sauce to thicken.
5. Stir in the tomato paste and cream, ensuring the sauce is smooth and well combined. At this point, the sauce should no longer be boiling.
6. Season with salt and pepper to taste.
7. (Optional) Garnish with freshly chopped parsley before serving for extra flavor and freshness.

SERVING: 6 PEOPLE **PREP:** 10 MINS **COOK:** 10 MINS

Paprika Soße

Paprika Sauce

This sauce was formerly called "Zigeuner Soße" but is now known as "Hungarian Style Paprika Sauce" due to the original term being offensive to Romani and Sinti people. The sauce has no connection to Romani cuisine.

A beloved German staple that's perfect with schnitzel (p. 66) and grilled meats or even as a pasta sauce.

Ingredients

- 3 bell peppers (red, yellow, and green) (about 500 g /1 lb)
- 2 onions, sliced
- 2 garlic cloves, finely minced
- 1 can (400 g / 14 oz) chopped tomatoes
- 100 g (3 ½ oz / ½ cup) gherkins (pickles, not the sweet variety), diced
- 200 ml (6 ¾ fl oz / ¾ cup) vegetable stock or broth
- 1 teaspoon tomato paste
- 2 tablespoon tomato ketchup
- 1 tablespoon vinegar (from the gherkin jar)
- 1 tablespoon sweet paprika powder
- ½ teaspoon chili powder
- 1 teaspoon sugar (optional)
- 1 tablespoon olive oil
- Fresh parsley (for serving)

Instructions

1. Slice bell peppers into thick strips. Avoid cutting too finely, as they should retain texture after cooking.
2. Slice onions and chop gherkins into 0.5 cm (¼ inch) chunks. Mince garlic.
3. Heat olive oil in a large skillet or saucepan over medium heat.
4. Add bell peppers and onions, sautéing until onions become translucent.
5. Stir in garlic, gherkins, and tomato paste, and fry briefly to release flavors.
6. Pour in canned tomatoes, vegetable stock (or broth), and ketchup.
7. Add paprika, chili powder, and vinegar, stirring well to combine.
8. Taste the sauce—if too acidic, balance with a little sugar.
9. Let sauce simmer over medium-low heat for about 5 minutes. (Peppers should be cooked but still slightly crunchy.)
10. Before serving, sprinkle with freshly chopped parsley for freshness.

SERVING: 8 PEOPLE **PREP:** 20 MIN **COOK:** 20 MIN

Apfelmus

Apple Sauce

A popular condiment often served as a side dish with savory foods, reflecting Germany's use of fruit in hearty meals. Make large batches and freeze the apple sauce in portions or can in sterilized jars whilst still hot.

Ingredients

- 1 kg (2 lb) tart apples
- 100 ml (½ cup) water
- 3 teaspoons vanilla extract (or substitute with the pulp of a vanilla pod)
- 2 tablespoons granulated sugar
- 1 cinnamon stick (can be substituted with ½ teaspoon ground cinnamon
- 2 tablespoons lemon juice

Instructions

1. Prepare by peeling and coring the apple. Quarter and slice into roughly 2 cm / 1 inch chunks.
2. Place all the apples with the water, vanilla extract, sugar, cinnamon, and lemon juice in the pot and bring to a boil on low to medium heat for approximately 15-20 minutes.
3. Stir occasionally to prevent the bottom of the pan from burning. Once the apples have softened and fallen apart, remove the cinnamon stick and vanilla beans (if using).
4. You can use a potato masher or an immersion blender to puree the apple sauce to the desired consistency.
5. Leave to cool or serve immediately.

To cook in a crockpot

1. Place all ingredients into the cooker and set the cooker on high.
2. Leave to boil for approx 4 hours. There is no need to stir the apples, as they cook slowly and the bottom will not burn.

To cook in a pressure cooker

1. Place all ingredients into the pressure cooker and cook for 5 minutes at high pressure.

More info at https://mydinner.co.uk/apfelmus/ or Google "*MyDinner Apfelmus*" .

Hauptgänge
MAIN COURSES

SERVING: 4 PEOPLE **PREP:** 30MINS **COOK:** 1 HR 30 MINS

Rindergulasch

Beef Goulash

This simple recipe has already won over so many of you. There's something magical about a beef goulash that's bursting with rich paprika flavor - it's comfort food at its finest. This foolproof version works every single time, making it perfect for both weeknight dinners and special occasions.

Ingredients

- 500 g stewing beef (1 lb), best cuts: beef chuck, shoulder, rib, topside or silverside.
- 4 tablespoons neutral oil (sunflower, or rapseed)
- 3 onions (about 250 g/ 9 oz)
- 1 garlic clove
- 2 tablespoons tomato paste
- 200 ml dry red wine (¾ cup) dry red wine
- 450 ml beef broth (2 cups)
- 1 teaspoon marjoram
- 1 tablespoon sweet paprika powder
- 1 teaspoon spicy paprika powder (optional)
- 1 teaspoon organic lemon zest
- 2 bay leaves
- salt and pepper
- 2 tablespoons cornflour/starch (optional)

Instructions

1. If needed, cut meat into 2–3 cm (1-inch) cubes for even cooking.
2. In a large saucepan, heat half the oil over high heat. Add the meat and sear until browned on all sides to develop rich flavor. If cooking a large quantity, fry in batches to prevent overcrowding, which causes steaming instead of searing. Once browned, remove and set aside.
3. Pour the remaining oil into the pan. Add the onions and sauté over medium heat until golden brown. Stir in the garlic and cook another minute, stirring frequently to prevent burning.
4. Stir in the tomato paste and cook about a minute to deepen flavor and color.
5. Deglaze the pan with red wine, scraping up browned bits. Let simmer until reduced by two-thirds.
6. Add paprika powders (sweet and spicy), marjoram, bay leaves, and lemon zest. Pour in the beef broth and season with salt and pepper.

More info at https://mydinner.co.uk/german-goulash/ or Google "*MyDinner German Goulash*" .

Rindergulasch

Beef Goulash

7. Cover the saucepan and let the goulash simmer gently for about 90 minutes, stirring occasionally.
8. After 60 minutes, check consistency. If too liquid, remove the lid for the last 30 minutes to reduce. Alternatively, mix 1 tablespoon cornstarch with 2 tablespoons water and stir in to thicken.

Slow Cooker / Crockpot Method

1. Follow the stovetop instructions up to Step 5.
2. Transfer the seared meat, onions, and cooked ingredients to the slow cooker.
3. Add the beef broth and wine to the slow cooker.
4. Cook on LOW for 5–6 hours or until the meat is fork-tender.
5. If the stew is too liquid, remove the lid for the last hour to help it reduce.
6. If necessary, stir in 1 tablespoon of cornstarch mixed with water, then bring to a boil to thicken.

Pressure Cooker Method

1. Follow the stovetop instructions up to Step 7.
2. Transfer the mixture to the pressure cooker. Secure the lid and cook at high pressure for 45 minutes.
3. Once done, release the pressure and remove the lid.
4. If the sauce is too thin, mix 1 tablespoon cornstarch with 2 tablespoon water, stir it in, and bring the stew to a gentle boil with the lid removed to thicken. Repeat if necessary.

SERVING: 4 PEOPLE **PREP:** 40 MINS **COOK:** 40 MINS

Königsberger Klopse

Meatballs in Caper Sauce

What fascinates me even more than the unique taste of these flavoursome, slightly sour meatballs, is their history. This traditional German dish originates from Königsberg—now known as Kaliningrad, Russia—which was once part of Prussia. You can read more about its fascinating history on my website.

Ingredients

For the Klopse / Meatballs

- 2 stale crusty rolls, preferably a day old
- 1 tablespoon butter
- 1 onion, finely chopped
- 250 g (9 oz) ground beef
- 250 g (9 oz) ground pork
- 1 egg
- 3 tablespoons breadcrumbs
- 2 teaspoons lemon zest
- 3 anchovies, finely chopped (optional). Alternatively, use ½ teaspoon anchovy paste.
- 1 teaspoon marjoram (if unavailable, use sage)
- Salt and pepper to taste

For the broth/stock

- 1 litre beef broth/stock 4 cups
- 1 bay leaf
- ½ teaspoon all spice
- 1 onion quartered

For the caper sauce

- 3 tablespoons butter
- 2 tablespoons all-purpose flour
- 1 pinch sugar
- 2 teaspoons lemon juice
- 350 ml (1 ½ cups) from the meatball broth/stock
- 150 ml (⅔ cup) cream, heavy or whipping cream
- 3 tablespoons capers
- Salt and pepper to taste

To serve

- 3 tablespoons parsley, finely chopped

More info at https://mydinner.co.uk/konigsberger-klopse/ or Google "*MyDinner Königsberger Klopse*".

Königsberger Klopse

Meatballs in Caper Sauce

To Make the Meatballs:

1. Soak the bread rolls in warm water for approximately 15 minutes. Once softened, squeeze out all excess liquid using a colander or cheesecloth. (This step is crucial to prevent the meatballs from becoming too soggy and falling apart.)
2. Finely chop the onion. Heat the butter in a frying pan and sauté the onions until translucent
3. In a large bowl, combine the ground meat, squeezed bread pulp, egg, breadcrumbs, lemon zest, marjoram, fried onions, and anchovy or anchovy paste (if using). Mix until a smooth and uniform mixture forms. Season with salt and pepper to taste.

To Make the Broth and Cook the Meatballs:

1. Prepare the broth: Place the beef broth, bay leaf, allspice, and quartered onion in a large pot. Bring to a boil, then reduce the heat to a simmer.
2. Carefully add the meatballs to the simmering broth (do not boil vigorously) and let them cook gently for 15–20 minutes.
3. Check that the largest meatball is fully cooked throughout before removing all meatballs from the broth.
4. Using a slotted spoon, transfer the cooked meatballs onto a plate.
5. Reserve 350 ml (1 ½ cups) of the broth for the sauce and set aside.

To Make the Sauce:

1. In a saucepan, melt the butter over medium heat.
2. Stir in the flour and cook, stirring continuously, until it forms a smooth paste (roux).
3. Slowly pour in the reserved broth, stirring constantly to prevent lumps. Bring to a boil and let it cook for about 5 minutes, allowing it to thicken.
4. Remove the pot from the heat, then stir in the drained capers and cream.
5. Add lemon juice, then season with salt, pepper, and a pinch of sugar to balance the flavors.

To Assemble:

1. Pour the sauce over the cooked meatballs. Garnish with freshly chopped parsley. Serve warm.

SERVING: 4 PEOPLE **PREP:** 30 MINS **COOK:** 1 HR 30 MINS

Rinderrouladen

Beef rouladen

A favorite Sunday roast—not just in my family. If you're worried the sauce won't taste like your mum's, don't be. This version blends rich roasting juices with pickle brine and cranberry sauce for a delicious sweet-and-sour flavor.

Ingredients

For the beef rouladen

- 900 g (2 lb) beef slices, sliced 1 cm thick (no thicker than ½ inch) (UK: use topside or silverside; USA: use beef round steaks)
- 12 cornichons, sliced into thin strips (or substitute dill pickles, sliced into thinner strips)
- 2 onions (200 g / 7 oz), halved and thinly sliced
- 4 teaspoons mustard (German mustard is ideal, but Dijon mustard works as a substitute)
- 4 slices streaky bacon
- 2 tablespoons neutral oil (such as vegetable or canola oil)
- Salt and pepper to taste

For the sauce

- 1 tablespoon vegetable oil
- 600 ml (2.5 cups / 20 fl oz) beef broth or stock
- 1 leek, sliced into thin rings
- 2 carrots (200 g / 7 oz), peeled and cubed
- 2 onions (200 g / 7 oz), peeled and cubed
- 2 cloves garlic, peeled and finely sliced
- 1 tablespoon tomato paste
- 375 ml (1.5 cups / 12.5 fl oz) dry red wine
- 2 tablespoons cranberry sauce, plus more to adjust taste
- 1 teaspoon dried thyme
- 2 bay leaves
- 2 tablespoons cornstarch (cornflour) mixed with 2 tablespoons water (for thickening smooth sauce)

More info at https://mydinner.co.uk/beef-rouladen/ or Google "*MyDinner GermanRouladen*" .

Rinderrouladen

Beef rouladen

Instructions

To Make the Beef Roulade

1. Slice the cornichons into thin strips. Peel and halve the onions, then slice them into thin strips.
2. Place each beef slice between two sheets of plastic wrap. Using the flat side of a meat mallet or the bottom of a heavy saucepan, pound the meat thin. This helps make it easier to roll later.
3. Season both sides of the meat with salt and pepper. Spread one teaspoon of mustard onto each slice.
4. Place one slice of bacon on top, followed by the cornichons and onion slices, alternating between them. Leave a 2 cm (¾ inch) edge if possible.
5. Roll the beef: First, fold in the long edges slightly to prevent the filling from falling out. Then roll it up tightly from the short side. If the beef slice is too narrow, skip folding the edges.
6. Secure each roulade with kitchen twine (wrapped like a present) or use toothpicks as an alternative.
7. If using an oven, preheat it to 180°C (356°F) with fan assistance.
8. Heat neutral oil in a large pan over high heat. Sear the roulades on all sides until browned—this enhances the flavor. If making multiple roulades, fry them in batches to avoid overcrowding. Remove from the pan and set aside.
9. Prepare the vegetables: Peel and cube the carrots and onions. Slice the leek into thin rings. Peel and finely slice the garlic.
10. In the same pan, heat 1 tablespoon of vegetable oil and sauté the vegetables over medium heat for about 5 minutes. Stir in the tomato paste and cook for another minute.
11. Deglaze the pan with red wine, allowing it to boil until reduced by half. Stir in the thyme, bay leaves, and cranberry sauce.

Choose One of the Following Cooking Methods:

Oven Method

1. Follow steps 1–11.
2. Place the covered pan in the preheated oven and cook for about 90 minutes.
3. Check every 30 minutes, turning the roulades to ensure even cooking.
4. If the sauce reduces too much, add more wine or broth to top it up.

Stovetop Method

1. Follow steps 1–11.
2. Simmer the roulades over low to medium heat for about 90 minutes.
3. Check every 30 minutes, turning them to ensure even cooking.
4. If needed, add more wine or broth to maintain the sauce consistency.

More info at https://mydinner.co.uk/beef-rouladen/ or Google "*My Dinner German Rouladen*" .

Rinderrouladen

Beef rouladen

Slow Cooker Method

1. Follow steps 1–11.
2. Transfer the roulades to the slow cooker and cover with the lid.
3. Cook on LOW for 7–8 hours or on HIGH for 4 hours.
4. Turn the roulades occasionally for even cooking.
5. Ensure they remain submerged in liquid. If needed, add broth, but do not add wine, as it will not get hot enough to cook off the alcohol.

To Make the Sauce

For a Thick Sauce:

1. Remove the bay leaves.
2. Using an immersion blender, blend the vegetables into a thick sauce.
3. Taste and adjust: Add more cranberry sauce for sweetness or, if it is too sweet, stir in one tablespoon of gherkin brine from the cornichon jar.
4. Season with salt and pepper to taste.

For a Smooth Sauce:

1. Remove the bay leaves.
2. Strain the vegetables and capture the liquid in a bowl. Discard the vegetables.
3. Place the liquid back onto the stove and bring to a boil.
4. Stir in the cornstarch and water mixture to thicken.
5. Taste and adjust: Add more cranberry sauce for sweetness or, if it is too sweet, stir in one tablespoon of gherkin brine from the cornichon jar.
6. Season with salt and pepper to taste.

Serve the warm roulades with potato dumplings, Spätzle, or German red cabbage. Drizzle the sauce generously over the roulades.

SERVING: 4 PEOPLE **PREP:** 30MINS **COOK:** 3 HRS **MARINATE:** 4 DAYS

Rheinischer Sauerbraten

Rhenish-Style Marinated Pot Roast

I was given this recipe by my neighbor, who comes from the Rhineland. It's a slow-marinated roast beef cooked in a delicious, sweet and sour gingerbread gravy—a beloved dish in German cuisine.

Ingredients

For the marinade

- 2 onions
- 2 carrots
- 100 g (3.5 oz) celeriac
- 30 g (1 oz) parsley
- 2 tablespoons brown sugar
- 50 ml (¼ cup / 1.7 fl oz) red wine vinegar
- ½ teaspoon allspice
- 6 juniper berries
- 1 tablespoon black peppercorns
- 5 cloves (the spice)
- 3 bay leaves
- 500 ml (2 cups / 16 fl oz) dry red wine

For the meat

- 1 kg (2lb) beef roast
- 3 tablespoons vegetable oil
- 2 tablespoons flour
- 2 tablespoons tomato paste
- 1 liter (4 cups / 34 fl oz) beef stock
- 60 g (2 oz) Lebkuchen or Biscoff biscuits
- 3 tablespoons raisins

More info at https://mydinner.co.uk/sauerbraten/ or Google *"MyDinner Sauerbraten"*.

Rheinischer Sauerbraten

Rhenish-Style Marinated Pot Roast

Instructions

To Marinate

1. Peel the onions, carrots, and celeriac, then chop them into 1.5 cm (½ inch) cubes. Roughly chop the parsley root.
2. Add the vegetables to a large saucepan. Stir in the brown sugar, allspice, juniper berries, peppercorns, cloves, and bay leaves. Then pour in the red wine.
3. Bring the mixture to a boil, then reduce to medium-low heat and let it simmer for 5 minutes to infuse the marinade with flavor.
4. Allow the marinade to cool completely to room temperature. Stir in the red wine vinegar.
5. Place the beef roast in a deep container with a lid. Pour the marinade over the beef, ensuring it is fully submerged. If needed, add a little water to submerge the meat. For best results, vacuum-seal the beef.
6. Cover and refrigerate for at least 4 days (ideally 7). Turn the beef once or twice during this time to ensure even marination.

To Cook

1. Remove the beef from the marinade and pat it dry with paper towels.
2. Strain the marinade through a fine sieve, reserving the liquid. Set aside the vegetables and spices separately.
3. Season the beef on all sides with salt and pepper. Lightly dust with flour.
4. In a large Dutch oven or heavy pot, heat the vegetable oil over high heat. Sear the beef on all sides for about 2 minutes per side, then remove it from the pot and set aside.
5. Preheat the oven to 170°C (340°F).
6. Add the drained vegetables and spices to the pot. Sauté for 2 minutes, then stir in the tomato paste and cook for another 2 minutes to enhance the flavor.
7. Deglaze the pot with a splash of the reserved marinade, just enough to cover the base of the pot. Cook until most of the liquid evaporates, then repeat this process one more time.
8. Pour in the beef stock and the remaining marinade. Return the beef roast to the pot.
9. Crumble the Lebkuchen or Biscoff biscuits into the sauce.
10. Cover with a lid and transfer to the oven. Cook for 2.5-3 hours, turning the meat at least once during cooking. The meat should be fork-tender when done.

Rheinischer Sauerbraten

Rhenish-Style Marinated Pot Roast

To Make the Sauce

1. Remove the beef from the pot, wrap it in foil, and set it aside to rest.
2. Strain the sauce through a fine sieve, then return it to the stovetop. Boil for 5 minutes to reduce.
3. Add the raisins and cook for another 10 minutes until the sauce thickens.

To Serve

1. Slice the beef into 1.5 cm (½ inch) thick slices.
2. Pour the rich sauce over the top.

SERVING: 4 PEOPLE **PREP:** 15 MINS **COOK:** 1 HR

Kohlrouladen

Cabbage Rolls

A meatball wrapped in braised cabbage and cooked in a seasoned broth. What is not to like? I make this recipe in batches and freeze them in portions. Try savoy cabbage instead of white or green cabbage for a different texture.

Ingredients

For the cabbage rolls

- 100 g (3.5 oz) stale or dry white bread (such as a bread roll or baguette)
- 450 g (1 lb) ground beef (or a 50/50 mix of beef and pork)
- 1 onion, finely chopped
- 2 medium eggs
- 1 teaspoon salt
- ¼ teaspoon black pepper
- 1 teaspoon mustard (such as Dijon mustard)
- 1 teaspoon sweet paprika powder
- 1 teaspoon marjoram
- 1 head of white, green, or Savoy cabbage
- 3 tablespoons vegetable oil

For the sauce

- 1 onion, chopped
- 2 carrots, chopped
- 1 tablespoon brown sugar
- 1 tablespoon tomato paste
- 750 ml (3 cups / 25 fl oz) beef stock
- 2 bay leaves
- 2 tablespoons cornstarch (optional, for thickening)

More info at https://mydinner.co.uk/cabbage-rolls/ or Google "*MyDinner Cabbage Rolls*" .

Kohlrouladen
Cabbage Rolls

Instructions

Prepare

1. Slice the bread into small pieces and soak them in warm water. Squeeze out any excess moisture to prevent the filling from becoming too wet.
2. In a large bowl, combine the ground beef, squeezed bread, finely chopped onion, eggs, salt, pepper, mustard, paprika, and marjoram. Knead the ingredients with your hands until well combined.
3. Prepare the cabbage leaves: Remove 8 large outer leaves from the cabbage head (the exact number depends on the size of your cabbage).
4. Bring a large pot of water to a boil. Blanch the cabbage leaves for 2–3 minutes to soften them. Remove them from the pot and pat them dry with a kitchen towel. (Avoid over-blanching, or the leaves may become too fragile and fall apart.)
5. Trim the cabbage leaves: Cut out the thick stem at the base of each leaf.
6. Divide the beef mixture into 8 equal portions. Lay a cabbage leaf flat and place one portion of the filling in the center.
7. Fold in the sides, then roll up the cabbage tightly. Secure each roll with kitchen twine to prevent them from unwrapping while cooking.

Cook

1. In a large pot, heat the vegetable oil over high heat. Sear the cabbage rolls (seam-side down first), browning them on all sides. Remove them from the pot and set aside.
2. In the same pot, reduce heat to medium and sauté the onions and carrots until the onions turn translucent.
3. Sprinkle in the brown sugar and cook until the onions and carrots caramelize.
4. Stir in the tomato paste and cook for 1 minute before pouring in the beef stock and adding the bay leaves.
5. Return the cabbage rolls to the pot, cover with a lid, and simmer on low heat for 45 minutes.

Finish the Sauce

1. Remove the cabbage rolls and bay leaves from the pot.
2. Boil the remaining cooking liquid, allowing it to reduce into a rich brown gravy.
3. To thicken the sauce (optional): Mix 1 tablespoon of cornstarch with 2 tablespoons of water, then stir the mixture into the boiling sauce. Repeat with another tablespoon of cornstarch if needed, until the sauce reaches your desired consistency. Season with salt and pepper to taste.

SERVING: 4 PEOPLE **PREP:** 10 MINS **COOK:** 30 MINS

Paprika Hähnchen

Paprika Chicken Drumsticks

This is a popular midweek dinner in our house. I always keep a jar of the chicken seasoning ready to go, by making a large batch and storing it in a jar. Use about 2 tablespoons for 1lb/ 500 gr of chicken. We usually serve it with mashed potatoes and a fresh & crispy green salad.

Ingredients

- 2 tablespoons sweet paprika powder
- 1 teaspoon garlic granules
- ½ teaspoon onion granules
- 1 teaspoon dried oregano
- 1 teaspoon dried parsley
- 1 teaspoon salt
- ¼ teaspoon ground black pepper

¼ teaspoon cayenne pepper (optional, for spice)

For the chicken

- 900 g (2 lb) chicken drumsticks

To serve

- 1 tablespoon fresh parsley chopped, optional

Instructions

1. In a small bowl or jar, combine all the seasoning ingredients and stir or shake until well blended.
2. Rub the seasoning mix generously over the chicken drumsticks. (If desired, brush the chicken with olive oil first, but this step is optional, as the skin contains enough fat.)
3. Cook the chicken using your preferred method:
4. Oven Method: Preheat the oven to 200°C (390°F). Place the drumsticks on a baking sheet and bake for 30 minutes, or until fully cooked.
5. Before serving, sprinkle with fresh parsley for extra flavor (if using).

More info at https://mydinner.co.uk/paprika-chicken/ or Google "*MyDinner Paprika Chicken*".

SERVING: 4 PEOPLE **PREP:** 30MINS **COOK:** 1 HR 30 MINS

Wiener Schnitzel

Breaded Veal Escalope

This is my go-to schnitzel recipe. Wiener Schnitzel is made with veal but you can also use the same method with turkey steaks or pork cutlets. Serve it with Spaetzle, Potato Salad or Bratkartoffeln. It's one of Germany's favorite foods. For the gravy lover - try it with Jäger Sauce (p. 47) or Rahmsauce (p. 48).

Ingredients

- 4 veal escalopes (veal cutlets), about 150 g (5 oz) each, cut to 5–7 mm (¼ inch) thick
- 2 tablespoons whipped cream (or substitute heavy/double cream)
- 2 medium eggs
- 75 g (½ cup / 1.7 oz) plain flour
- 150 g (1 cup / 5 oz) breadcrumbs
- 240 ml (1 cup / 8 fl oz) neutral oil (such as vegetable, canola, or rapeseed oil)
- 2 tablespoons butter
- Salt and pepper to taste

To Serve

- 1 lemon, sliced

Instructions

1. Tenderize the meat: Place a veal cutlet between two sheets of plastic wrap (or use a cut-up freezer bag). Using a meat mallet (smooth side) or a heavy pan, pound the meat until it is 4–5 mm (⅛ inch) thin. Repeat with the remaining veal cutlets.
2. Prepare the breading station: Place the flour on a large plate and season it with salt and pepper. In a wide, shallow bowl, whisk the eggs with the whipped cream until well combined. Spread the breadcrumbs onto a third plate. (When arranged in order—flour, egg wash, and breadcrumbs—this setup is called "Schnitzelstraße" ("Schnitzel Street").)
3. Bread the schnitzel: First lightly coat a veal escalope in the flour, shaking off any excess. Then dip it into the egg mixture, ensuring it is fully coated. Finally, coat the veal with breadcrumbs, pressing gently to help them adhere.
4. Cook the schnitzel: In a large frying pan, heat the oil and butter over medium heat. The oil should fully cover the bottom of the pan and be deep enough for the schnitzel to "swim" in it. Fry the schnitzel in batches for 2–3 minutes per side, until golden brown. While frying, use a spoon to continuously baste the schnitzel with oil— which helps create the classic wavy texture.
5. Drain and serve: Transfer the schnitzel to a paper towel-lined plate to drain any excess oil. Serve immediately with a slice of lemon.

SERVING: 4 PEOPLE **PREP:** 10 MINS **COOK:** 20 MINS

Cordon Bleu Schnitzel

Breaded Escalope Stuffed with Cheese and Ham

Cordon Bleu is like Schnitzel but on steroids. It is stuffed with ham and cheese. And never fails to impress. You can read the interesting history behind this dish on the website. Serve it with a side of fries or spätzle and a green salad.

Ingredients

- 4 pork loin chops or pork leg cuts, about 150 g–200 g (5–7 oz) each. Alternatively, use veal cutlets.
- 5 tablespoons all-purpose flour
- 2 medium eggs
- 2 tablespoons whipping cream (optional)
- 150 g (5 ½ oz, 2 ½ cups) breadcrumbs
- 90 ml (½ cup, 4 fl oz) neutral oil
- 1 tablespoon butter
- 4 slices (about 100 g/ 3 ½ oz,) cooked ham
- 4 slices (about 100 g/ 3 ½ oz) Emmental or Gouda cheese
- Salt and black pepper to taste

Instructions

Prepare the Breading Station:

- Line up three deep bowls. In the first bowl, add the flour.
- In the second bowl, crack the eggs, whisk them together with the cream (optional), and season with salt and pepper.
- In the third bowl, place the breadcrumbs

.

Prepare the Meat:

- Rinse the meat and pat it dry with a kitchen towel.
- Place it between two sheets of plastic wrap (a cut-up freezer bag works well). Using a meat mallet (smooth side) or the bottom of a heavy pan, pound the meat to about 4 mm (1/8 inch) thickness.
- Season the schnitzel on both sides with salt and pepper.
- (Optional step for perfect presentation): If desired, fold the schnitzel in half to create a perfect rectangle and trim off excess edges. (I personally skip this step to avoid unnecessary waste.)

More info at https://mydinner.co.uk/cordon-bleu/ or Google "*MyDinner Cordon Bleu Schnitzel*".

Cordon Bleu Schnitzel

Breaded Escalope Stuffed with Cheese and Ham

Assemble the Cordon Bleu:

1. Fold the schnitzel in half and fill with ham and cheese. Ensure that you leave a 1 cm/ ½ inch border around the edges.
2. Now hammer with the meat mallet around the edges of the schnitzel pocket. This should bind the edges without the need to use toothpicks or cooking twine. If you find that your cordon bleu still falls apart, you can secure the edges with toothpicks, but in my experience it is not necessary.

Bread the Schnitzel:

1. First, dredge the schnitzel in the flour, making sure both sides are evenly coated.
2. Next, dip the schnitzel into the egg mixture, ensuring full coverage, then letting any excess drip off.
3. Lastly, coat the schnitzel in breadcrumbs, pressing lightly to ensure the coating adheres well.

Cook the Schnitzel:

1. Heat the clarified butter or oil in a frying pan. The optimal frying temperature is 170°C (338°F). There should be enough oil in the pan so that the schnitzel can "swim" in the fat.
2. Fry each schnitzel for about 4–6 minutes per side, until golden brown and crispy.
3. Serve immediately while hot and crispy.

SERVING: 4 PEOPLE **PREP:** 10 MINS **COOK:** 10 MINS

Käsespätzle

Egg Dumplings with Cheese Sauce

A friend once asked me, "If you could eat one food for the rest of your life, what would it be?" My answer wasn't cake or dessert—it was Käsespätzle. These soft egg dumplings, served in an aromatic, creamy cheese sauce and topped with crispy onions, are my absolute favorite. I hope you enjoy them as much as I do.

Ingredients

- 250 g (9 oz, 2 cups) shop-bought spätzle (as an alternative if you do not want to make them from scratch)

To Make Homemade Spätzle:

- 3 medium eggs, at room temperature
- 100 ml (½ cup, 3.5 fl oz) milk
- 1 tablespoon unsalted butter, melted
- ½ teaspoon salt
- 250 g (2 cups, 9 oz) all-purpose flour

Caramelized Onions:

- 2 onions (about 250 g / ½ lb)
- 2 tablespoons flour
- 2 tablespoons butter
- 1 tablespoon vegetable oil

To Assemble

- 125 g (1 cups, 4.5 oz) grated cheese (Emmental or Bergkäse are traditional, but alternatives include Swiss or Cheddar)
- 100 ml (½ cup, 3.5 fl oz) whipping cream or heavy cream (double cream)
- Nutmeg, salt, and black pepper to taste

To Serve:

- 1 bunch chives, finely chopped (optional)

More info at https://mydinner.co.uk/kaesespaetzle/or Google "*MyDinner Cheese Spaetzle*" .

Käsespätzle

Egg Dumplings with Cheese Sauce

To Make the Spätzle from Scratch

1. In a mixing bowl, combine the eggs, salt, milk, and melted butter.
2. Sift the flour over the top, then immediately beat everything together into a loose dough using a wooden spoon, hand mixer, or stand mixer. Continue mixing until the dough bubbles and gains elasticity.
3. Let the dough rest for 10 minutes to allow the gluten to develop. (In the meantime, start preparing the onions —see below.)
4. Bring a large saucepan of salted water to a boil.
5. Using your spätzle maker of choice, slowly pour in the dough and press the strands into the boiling water.
6. The spätzle will rise to the top once they are cooked. Use a slotted spoon to remove them. Avoid overcrowding to prevent them from sticking.

- *Alternative: Using Store-Bought Spätzle*
- *Prepare dry Spätzle according to the package instructions.*

Make the Caramelized Onions

- Peel and thinly slice the onions into strips.
- Toss them with flour—this helps create a crispy texture.
- In a frying pan, melt the butter with 1 tablespoon of vegetable oil over medium heat.
- Fry the onions over low to medium heat until they become golden brown and crispy.
- Drain the onions on a paper towel to remove excess oil.

To Assemble

- Reduce the heat of in the same frying pan used for the onions.
- Add the warm, cooked spätzle to the pan.
- Sprinkle with grated cheese and a few small splashes of cream. Stir continuously until the cheese melts and coats the spätzle.
- Season with nutmeg (optional), salt, and pepper to taste.
- Before serving, sprinkle with chopped chives.

SERVING: 4 PEOPLE **PREP:** 25 MINS **COOK:** 10 MINS

Frikadellen

Fried Meat Patties

Creating a piece of Germany from anywhere in the world is shockingly simple, when you're using this Frikadellen recipe. You can make large ones which resemble mini meatloves or smaller snack-sized ones. But no matter the size , they will be gone in no time. They taste great hot or cold.

Ingredients

- 500 g (1 lb) ground pork (or substitute with ground beef)
- 500 g (1 lb) ground beef
- 1 stale crusty roll (100 g / 3.5 oz) white bread or baguette
- 1 medium egg
- 1 onion (70 g / 2.4 oz), peeled and finely sliced
- 1 tablespoon vegetable or sunflower oil (for frying the onion)
- 1 teaspoon mustard
- 1 teaspoon salt
- 1 teaspoon black pepper
- 1 teaspoon ground sweet paprika
- 1 teaspoon dried marjoram (or substitute with sage)
- 1 teaspoon dried parsley (or substitute with fresh parsley)
- Butter, clarified butter, or vegetable oil (for frying the meatballs)

Instructions

1. Soak the bread roll in a bowl of water. Once it softens, squeeze out the excess liquid using your hands, a spoon, or a sieve. This step is important, as too much moisture will affect the texture of the meatballs.
2. Fry the sliced onion in a frying pan with 1 tablespoon of oil until it starts to brown.
3. In a large bowl, combine the ground meat, bread pulp, fried onion, egg, mustard, salt, pepper, marjoram, parsley, and paprika. Knead the mixture with your hands or a wooden spoon until everything is thoroughly combined.
4. Roll a small test meatball and fry it in oil to check the seasoning. Taste and adjust if needed.
5. Form meatballs with your hands. Using an ice cream scoop helps portion them evenly. (Each should be about 5 cm in diameter and weigh approximately 50 g / 1.7 oz.)
6. Heat a frying pan over medium heat and add enough oil or clarified butter to cover the base. Fry the meatballs for 5–7 minutes per side.
7. Do not turn the meatballs too early; let them fry undisturbed to develop a firmer and crispier texture, preventing them from breaking apart.

More info at https://mydinner.co.uk/german-beef-meatballs/or Google *"MyDinner Frikadellen"* .

Frikadellen

Fried Meat Patties

8. Ensure the oil is not too hot; otherwise, the outside will crisp too quickly while the inside remains raw.
9. Place the cooked meatballs on a paper towel to absorb excess fat before serving.

To Make in the Oven

1. Preheat the oven to 200°C (392°F).
2. Place the meatballs on a baking tray lined with parchment paper.
3. Bake for 30–40 minutes, depending on size. Flip halfway through to ensure even cooking.

SERVING: 6 PEOPLE **PREP:** 15 MINS **COOK:** 15 MINS

Hühnerfrikassee

Chicken Fricassee

A favorite recipe of my children, who love the creamy texture of this dish. It's also one of my preferred ways to use up leftover chicken. Sometimes I adapt the recipe by substituting fresh vegetables with canned ones, making this a really speedy dinner. We usually serve it with rice.

Ingredients

- 350 g (¾ lb, 12oz) boneless chicken. You can also use leftover roast chicken.
- 250 g (9 oz) mushrooms
- 200 g (7 oz) carrots
- 150 g (5 oz) frozen peas
- 200 g (7 oz) asparagus
- 800 ml (3 ½ cups, 27 fl oz) chicken broth
- 60 g (½ cup, 2 oz) all-purpose flour
- 60 g (¼ cup, 2 oz) butter
- 90 ml (⅓ cup, 3 fl oz) whipping cream
- 1 egg yolk
- 1 splash lemon juice
- Salt and pepper to taste

Instructions

If Using Uncooked Chicken:

1. Cook the chicken: Place it in a pot of water with a little vegetable stock and boil until fully cooked. (Reserve the stock to use as for sauce later.)
2. Remove and discard the skin, then carefully take the meat off the bones.
3. Cut the cooked chicken into bite-sized pieces and set aside.

Preparing the Vegetables:

1. Peel and chop the carrots into 1 cm (½ inch) cubes.
2. Wash the mushrooms and slice them. For white asparagus: Peel and trim off the woody ends. For green asparagus: Just trim off the woody ends.
3. If using white asparagus, blanch it in hot water with a pinch of salt and sugar for 2 minutes. Green asparagus can be cooked straight in the stew.
4. Weigh the peas and prepare the chicken broth for later use.

More info at https://mydinner.co.uk/chicken-fricassee/ or Google "*MyDinner Chicken Fricassee*".

Hühnerfrikassee

Chicken Fricassee

Preparing Sauce Base:

1. Melt the butter in a saucepan over medium heat.
2. Add the flour, whisking continuously for a couple of minutes until it turns a golden-yellow color.
3. Slowly pour in small amounts of the stock/broth, whisking constantly to keep it smooth.

Cooking the Fricassee:

1. Stir in the cream, followed by the mushrooms, carrots, asparagus, and peas.
2. Allow to simmer on medium heat for about 8 minutes, until the vegetables are tender.
3. Carefully add the egg yolk, stirring quickly to incorporate it into the sauce.
4. Season with salt, pepper, and lemon juice to taste.
5. Gently fold in the cooked chicken and let it warm through in the sauce for 5 minutes. (The sauce should not be boiling at this stage.)

SERVING: 6 PEOPLE **PREP:** 20 MINS **COOK:** 45 MINS

Hackbraten

Meatloaf

Time for an uncomplicated family recipe. The first time I made this roast, I was shocked by how easily it comes together. Just mix the ingredients, form the meatloaf and place it in the even. Serve with Rahmsauce (p. 48) or Jägersauce. (p. 47)

Ingredients

- 800 g (28 oz) ground meat (50% pork, 50% beef) (*You can use only beef, but this will alter the texture.*)
- 2 stale bread rolls (*or stale baguette, about 100 g [3.5 oz]*)
- 1 medium onion (150 g [5 oz])
- 70 g (2.5 oz) pickled gherkins (*or cornichons; use dill pickles for best flavor*)
- 15 g (0.5 oz) fresh parsley, chopped
- 2 medium eggs
- 1 ½ teaspoons salt
- 1 teaspoon ground black pepper
- 1 teaspoon mustard
- 1 teaspoon sweet paprika powder
- 100 g (3.5 oz) butter

Instructions

1. Finely chop the onions, gherkins, and parsley.
2. Heat 1 tablespoon of butter in a pan and fry the onions until they start to brown.
3. In a large bowl, combine the ground meat, soaked bread, fried onions, eggs, mustard, gherkins, paprika powder, salt, and pepper. Mix thoroughly with your hands until combined.
4. Preheat your oven to 180°C (356°F). Lightly grease the bottom of an oven dish with butter.
5. Transfer the meat mixture into the prepared dish and shape it into an oval loaf.
6. Place the meatloaf in the oven and bake for approximately 45 minutes.
7. Melt the remaining butter in a pan or microwave. Every 10 minutes, brush with butter to help it brown.
8. To check for doneness, insert a meat thermometer into the center. If the internal temperature reaches 75°C (170°F), the meatloaf is fully cooked.
9. While the meatloaf is baking, prepare a quick sauce to serve with it. (Rahmsauce or Jägersauce are great options.)
10. Serve immediately. This meatloaf pairs with mashed potatoes, potato dumplings, and boiled vegetables.

More info at https://mydinner.co.uk/german-meatloaf/ or Google "*MyDinner German Meatloaf*".

SERVING: 1 **PREP:** 15 MINS **COOK:** 25 MINS

Flammkuchen

Bacon Flat Bread

There are two camps in our family. Team Pizza and Team Flammkuchen. I fall into the latter category. This crispy thin flatbread topped with sour cream, onions and crispy bacon wins every time for me. In Germany you will find entire restaurants dedicated to this dish.

I often serve this dish as fingerfood at parties. Everyone loves it.

Ingredients

- 2 tablespoons olive oil
- 120 ml (½ cup / 4 fl oz) water
- 1 pinch salt
- 250 g (2 cups / 9 oz) flour

For the Traditional Topping:

- 2 onions (abot 150 gr / 5 oz)
- 100 g (3.5 oz) bacon
- 60 ml (¼ cup, 2 fl oz) crème fraîche or substitute with full-fat Greek yogurt
- 60 ml (¼ cup / 2 fl oz) sour cream
- Black pepper to taste
- Salt, to taste
- 2 tablespoons chopped chives (optional)

Vegetarian Variation

- 100 g (3.5 oz) spinach
- 100 g (3.5 oz) cherry tomatoes
- 50 g (1.7 oz) onion
- 1 garlic clove
- 100 g (3.5 oz) feta cheese
- 60 ml (¼ cup, 2 fl oz) or substitute with full-fat Greek yogurt
- 60 ml (¼ cup , 2 fl oz) sour cream
- Salt and black pepper to taste

Smoked Salmon Variation

- 60 ml (¼ cup, 2 fl oz) or substitute with full-fat Greek yogurt
- 60 ml (¼ cup, 2 fl oz) sour cream
- 4 oz smoked salmon
- ¼ cup spring onions or rocket leaves

More info at https://mydinner.co.uk/flammkuchen-recipe/ or Google "*MyDinner Flammerkuchen*".

Flammkuchen

Bacon Flat Bread

Instructions

Preparing the Dough

1. Preheat the oven to 250°C (482°F).
2. In a mixing bowl, whisk together the water, olive oil, salt, and flour using a hand or stand mixer fitted with a dough hook or paddle attachment.
3. Turn the dough out onto a lightly floured surface.
4. Using a rolling pin, roll the dough into a thin sheet, approximately 3 mm thick. Transfer the dough to a sheet of baking parchment.

Traditional Flammkuchen Topping (Elsässer Art)

Preparing the Onions:

1. Slice the onions very finely and place them in a bowl with a little water.
2. Steam them in the microwave for about 1 minute at 600 watts. *(This step softens them and prevents the onions from burning too quickly.)*
3. In a bowl, mix the crème fraîche and sour cream until combined. Season with salt and pepper and set aside.
4. Spread the crème fraîche-sour cream mixture evenly over the dough using the back of a spoon, leaving a 0.5 cm border around the edges.
5. Evenly distribute the onions and bacon on top.
6. Place the Flammkuchen in the oven and bake for 10–15 minutes. *(Since every oven is different, keep an eye on it to prevent burning or over-crisping.)*
7. The Flammkuchen is ready when the edges turn crisp and golden brown. Remove from the oven and check if the center is cooked through.
8. To serve, sprinkle with chopped chives and serve warm.

Flammkuchen

Bacon Flat Bread

Vegetarian Variation:

1. Blanch the spinach in hot water, then squeeze out the excess liquid.
2. Slice the cherry tomatoes in half. Slice the onion and garlic. Cube the feta cheese.
3. In a bowl, mix the crème fraîche and sour cream until combined. Season with salt and pepper.
4. Spread the crème fraîche-sour cream mixture over the dough, leaving a 0.5 cm border around the edges.
5. Evenly distribute the spinach, cherry tomatoes, onion, garlic, and feta on top.
6. Bake until the edges crisp up and the topping is cooked through.

Smoked Salmon Variation

1. In a bowl, mix the crème fraîche and sour cream until combined. Season with salt and pepper.
2. Spread the crème fraîche-sour cream mixture over the dough, leaving a 0.5 cm border around the edges.
3. Bake in the hot oven for 10–15 minutes.
4. Once baked, evenly distribute the smoked salmon flakes over the hot Flammkuchen.
5. To serve, sprinkle with thinly sliced spring onion or rocket leaves.

SERVING: 4 PEOPLE **PREP:** 15 MINS **COOK:** 1 HR

Bratwurst Auflauf

Bratwurst Casserole

Let me introduce you to the ultimate bratwurst casserole dish. If you are looking for a meal that is hearty, spicy, and filling, you're in the right place. This dish has it all - braised cabbage, fried potato, crispy bacon, and of course the spiced sausage. Pair this with a green salad for a delicious wholesome meal.

Ingredients

- 4–6 bratwurst
- 450 g (1 lb) potatoes
- 800 g (1 3/4 lb) white cabbage
- 1 red bell pepper
- 2 tablespoons vegetable oil
- 75 g (2.5 oz or ⅓ cup) smoked bacon, cubed
- 1 ½ teaspoons dried sage
- ½ teaspoon caraway seeds (optional)
- 120 ml (½ cup or 4 fl oz) water
- Salt and pepper to taste

Instructions

1. Preheat the oven to 200°C (392°F).
2. Peel the potatoes and wash the cabbage and red bell pepper. Deseed the pepper, then chop all vegetables into roughly 2 cm / 1⁄2 inch pieces.
3. Heat vegetable oil in a large frying pan over medium heat. Add the bacon cubes and fry until crispy. Remove from the pan and set aside.
4. Place the sausages in the pan and fry on each side until browned. Remove and set aside with the bacon.
5. In the same pan, add the cabbage and potatoes and fry for 5–7 minutes in the bacon and sausage fat.
6. Season with sage, caraway seeds (if using), salt, and pepper. Mix well, then pour in the water to deglaze the pan.
7. In an ovenproof casserole dish, combine the red pepper, crispy bacon, and the cabbage-potato mixture.
8. Place the sausages on top, then cover with a lid.
9. Bake in the preheated oven for approximately 60 minutes, allowing the flavors to infuse.
10. Sprinkle with chopped spring onions before serving (optional).

More info at https://mydinner.co.uk/the-ultimate-bratwurst-casserole-with-cabbage-potatoes/ or Google *"MyDinner Bratwurst Casserole"*.

SERVING: 4 PEOPLE **PREP:** 30 MINS **COOK:** 10 MINS **REST:** 30 MINS

Gemüsestrudel

Vegetable Strudel

This vegetable strudel has become my go-to recipe when I need something comforting yet elegant. The golden, flaky pastry wrapped around tender broccoli, carrots, and zucchini manages to convince even my children to eat their veg. It's perfect for using up whatever vegetables are lurking in the fridge, and the store-bought puff pastry makes it perfect for busy weeknights.

Ingredients

- 1 tablespoon olive oil
- 2 onions, about 150g / 5 oz
- 2 garlic cloves
- 2 carrots, about 200g /7 oz
- 1 broccoli head, cut into florets, about 200g / 7 oz
- 1 zucchini, about 200g / 7 oz
- 2 large eggs (separated - you'll use 1 whole egg plus 1 egg yolk)
- 2 tablespoons cream cheese
- 1 ready-rolled puff pastry sheet, about 300g /10.5 oz - alternatively use a frozen block, defrost and roll out to a rectangle
- Salt and pepper to taste

Instructions

1. Peel the onions, carrots and garlic. Finely cube the onions and garlic and slice the carrots and zucchini into rounds. Chop the broccoli into florets.
2. Heat oil in a saucepan and fry the onions until translucent. Add the garlic and fry for 1 minute. Add the carrots and broccoli, cover and steam for 5 minutes. Add the zucchini and steam for 3 minutes. Vegetables should have bite.
3. Remove the vegetables from the heat and cool to room temperature.
4. Preheat oven to 200°C (392°F).
5. Separate one egg. Mix the egg white into the cooled vegetables with the cream cheese. Season with salt and pepper.
6. Unroll the puff pastry on the work surface. Add the vegetable filling in a mound. Brush egg yolk on the corners to secure ends.
7. Fold the dough over the vegetables and seal the ends tightly.
8. Turn the strudel seam-side down on a parchment-lined baking tray. Prick the top with a fork and score a decorative pattern if desired.
9. Brush with the remaining egg yolk and bake for 30 minutes until golden brown.

More info at https://mydinner.co.uk/vegetable-strudel/ or Google "*MyDinner Vegetable Strudel*".

SERVING: 4 PEOPLE **PREP:** 10 MINS **COOK:** 30 MINS

Würstchengulasch

Sausage Goulash

Frankfurt sausages are perfect for making any dish more exciting. Würstchengulasch is a tasty sausage stew typically made using leftovers. It's especially popular with kids. At home, we serve it with pasta and a big bowl of salad on the side.

Ingredients

- 5 Frankfurter sausages
- 100 g (3 ½ oz) bacon
- 1 onion
- 1 garlic clove
- 2 tablespoons tomato paste
- 1 bell pepper (red, green, or yellow)
- 350 g (12 oz) mushrooms
- 1 can (400 g / 14 oz) tomatoes
- 500 ml (2 cups / 16.9 fl oz) vegetable stock
- 100 g (3 ½ oz / ½ cup) whipping cream
- 1 tablespoon sunflower or olive oil

Spices

- 1 teaspoon sweet paprika
- ½ teaspoon spicy paprika (optional)
- ½ teaspoon rosemary
- ½ teaspoon thyme
- ½ teaspoon ground caraway seeds
- Salt and pepper to taste
- 1 teaspoon sugar

Instructions

1. Finely chop the bacon. Slice the sausages and mushrooms. Finely chop the onion and garlic. Roughly chop the bell pepper.
2. Heat the oil in a large pan over medium heat. Add the bacon and fry until browned and slightly crispy.
3. Stir in the sliced sausage, onion, mushrooms, and garlic, frying until the onions become translucent and start to brown slightly.
4. Add the bell pepper and continue frying for about 3 minutes.
5. Stir in the tomato paste and fry for an additional 2 minutes, allowing it to deepen in color and enhance the flavor.
6. Pour in the canned tomatoes, stirring well to combine. Then add the vegetable stock and bring to a gentle boil over medium-low heat. Let simmer for 20 minutes.
7. Season with salt, pepper, sugar, and spices to taste.
8. Stir in the cream and let it simmer for another 5 minutes. Taste and adjust seasoning if necessary.

lore info at https://mydinner.co.uk/sausage-goulash/or Google "*MyDinner Sausage Goulash*".

SERVING: 4 PEOPLE **PREP:** 30 MINS **COOK:** 10 MINS **REST:** 30 MINS

Maultaschen

Stuffed Pasta Pockets

This is one of my favorite Swabian recipes, a region that is famous for its down-to earth fare. A pasta pocket stuffed with spiced meat and sausages. I love to eat these in a rich broth, or fried in the pan with some eggs. These Maultaschen freeze really well, so I often double or triple the ingredients and make a big batch because my children love them.

Ingredients

For the Pasta Dough

- 300 g (2 ½ cups) flour
- 2 eggs
- 1 tablespoon oil
- 1 teaspoon salt

For the Maultaschen Filling

- 1 bread roll (a crusty roll is traditional, but you can substitute it with stale baguette)
- 1 tablespoon butter or oil
- 200 g (7 oz) spinach
- 1 onion, finely chopped
- 1 garlic clove, minced
- 200 g (7 oz) bratwurst meat, removed from casing

For the Filling

- 90 g (3 oz) ground beef
- 90 g (3 oz) ground pork
- 1 teaspoon marjoram
- 1 teaspoon salt
- ¼ teaspoon pepper
- 1 pinch nutmeg
- 1 teaspoon parsley, finely chopped
- 2 eggs

More info at https://mydinner.co.uk/maultaschen/ or Google "*MyDinner Maultaschen*".

Maultaschen

Stuffed Pasta Pockets

Instructions

Make the Pasta Dough

1. On a clean work surface, add the flour and salt, shaping it into a pile.
2. Use a spoon or your hands to create a well in the center, then crack the eggs into it. Pour in the oil.
3. Using a fork, gently beat the eggs and oil, gradually incorporating a little flour at a time.
4. Once the mixture becomes dense enough, begin kneading the dough by hand.
5. If the mixture is too moist, add some more flour. If it is too dry, add a teaspoon of water at a time.
6. Knead the dough until it is smooth and elastic.
7. Wrap the dough in cling film and refrigerate for at least 30 minutes to allow the gluten to develop.

Prepare the Filling

1. Soak the bread roll in warm water until soft, then squeeze out the excess water.
2. Blanch the spinach in hot water for about 2 minutes, then drain thoroughly.
3. Peel and finely chop the onion and garlic.
4. Heat 1 tablespoon of butter in a pan, then sauté the onion and garlic until soft and translucent. Set aside to cool.
5. In a large bowl, combine the ground beef, ground pork, bratwurst meat, soaked bread pulp, spinach, onion, garlic, marjoram, salt, pepper, parsley, nutmeg, and eggs.
6. Mix thoroughly with your hands until everything is evenly combined.

Assemble

- Using a rolling pin (or a pasta maker, if available), roll out the dough to about 3 mm (⅛ inch) thickness.
- Cut the dough into 15 cm (6 inch) squares using a sharp knife.
- Place a generous tablespoon of filling in the center of each square.
- Fold the dough over to create a pocket, then press the edges firmly with a fork to seal and create a decorative pattern.

Maultaschen

Stuffed Pasta Pockets

Cook

- In a large pot, bring the beef broth to a boil, then reduce the heat to a gentle simmer.
- Carefully place the Maultaschen into the simmering broth and cook for about 10 minutes.

Serve

- Serve immediately in the broth, garnished with chopped spring onions (green onions).
- Alternatively, fry the Maultaschen on all sides until golden brown—they also taste great with crispy fried onions on top!

SERVING: 4 PEOPLE **PREP:** 10 MINS **COOK:** 2 HRS

Biergulasch

Beerstew

With this stew, you combine the best of both worlds—the malty flavor of beer with hearty beef. I prefer a dark lager for this goulash, but you can also use a stout like Guinness if you prefer. Serve it with some Bread Dumplings (p. 33) and Red Cabbage (p. 35) on the side.

Ingredients

- 750 g (1.6 lb) diced beef
- 750 g (1.6 lb) diced pork
- 500 ml (2 cups) dark German beer (see post for substitutes)
- 750 ml (3 cups) beef stock
- 1 kg (2 lb) onions, diced
- 2 tablespoons butter
- 2 tablespoons tomato paste
- 3 teaspoons sweet paprika powder
- 1 teaspoon caraway seeds
- 2 tablespoons cornstarch / cornflour or plain flour
- Salt and pepper to taste

Instructions

Saucepan Method

1. Roughly dice the onions.
2. In a large saucepan (at least 5 liters), melt the butter over medium heat and fry the onions until soft and translucent.
3. Add the meat and fry until lightly browned.
4. Stir in the salt, pepper, paprika, tomato paste, and caraway seeds, and fry for another minute, stirring continuously.
5. Pour in the beef stock and beer, then reduce the heat to low.
6. Let it simmer on low heat for about 1 ½ to 2 hours, or until the meat is tender.
7. To thicken the goulash sauce, stir in 1 tablespoon of cornstarch/ cornflour or plain flour. Increase the heat slightly to activate the thickening process.

More info at https://mydinner.co.uk/german-pork-and-beef-beer-goulash/ or Google "*MyDinner Beergoulash*".

Biergulasch

Beerstew

Slow Cooker Method

1. Prepare the beer goulash following the stovetop instructions up to step 4.
2. Transfer the sautéed ingredients into your slow cooker or crockpot.
3. Add the beef stock and beer, then set your slow cooker or crockpot to HIGH.
4. Cook for about 5–6 hours on high, or until the meat falls apart easily with a fork.
5. To thicken the goulash sauce, stir in 1 tablespoon of cornstarch/ cornflour or plain flour and increase the heat slightly.

Pressure Cooker Method

1. Prepare the beer goulash following the stovetop instructions up to step 5.
2. Transfer the mixture to a pressure cooker, secure the lid and cook at high pressure for 45 minutes.
3. Once the lid is removed, stir in 1 tablespoon of cornstarch/ cornflour to thicken the sauce.
4. Bring the goulash back to a boil with the lid removed to help thicken the sauce.

SERVING: 4 PEOPLE **PREP:** 10 MINS **COOK:** 10 MINS

Currywurst

Bratwurst with Curry-seasoned Ketchup

For many Germans, when they think of fast food, Currywurst springs to mind. You'll find it everywhere, typically served from small huts. We have the British and Americans to thank for this dish, as they introduced curry powder and ketchup to Germany after the war. Every Currywurst stand has its secret recipe—but I'll share mine.

Ingredients

- 6 Bratwurst or Bockwurst

For the sauce

- 1 tablespoon olive oil
- 1 small onion, finely diced
- 1 clove garlic, minced
- 4 ½ tablespoons brown sugar
- 2 tablespoons tomato paste
- 1 can (400g/ 14 oz) diced tomatotes
- 1 teaspoon cider vinegar
- 1 teaspoon Worcestershire sauce
- 2 teaspoons mild curry powder
- 1 teaspoon cayenne pepper
- Salt and pepper to taste

Instructions

Prepare the Currywurst Sausages

1. Fry, barbecue, or grill the sausages until they are browned on all sides.

Make the sauce

1. In a pan, heat the olive oil over medium heat, then fry the onion and garlic until the onion becomes translucent.
2. Add the brown sugar and stir until the sugar crystals dissolve and the onion starts to caramelize.
3. Stir in the tomato paste and fry for one more minute.
4. Pour in the cider vinegar, followed by the tinned tomatoes. Bring to a simmer and let it boil until reduced by one-third.
5. Season with Worcestershire sauce, curry powder, and cayenne pepper.
6. Use an immersion blender to puree the tomato sauce until smooth.
7. Season with salt and pepper to taste.

Serve:

Slice your sausages and cover them in the sauce. Sprinkle extra turmeric on top for garnish and serve with a crusty roll or some fries on the side.

More info at https://mydinner.co.uk/currywurst-sauce/ or Google *"MyDinner Currywurst"*.

SERVING: 4 PEOPLE **PREP:** 10 MINS **COOK:** 20 MINS

Schmorkohl mit Hack

Braised Cabbage with Ground Beef

Some of the best recipes in my repertoire were born out of convenience and this dish is one of those. It's a leftover recipe that quickly turned into my son's favorite comfort meal. Shredded cabbage with ground beef- simple, inexpensive and utterly moreish. We serve it with boiled potatoes and rice.

Ingredients

- 1 kg (2.2 lbs) green, white, or Savoy cabbage
- 200 g (7 oz) onions (about 2 medium onions, finely chopped)
- 2 cloves garlic, minced
- 2 tablespoons vegetable oil
- 450 g (1 lb) ground beef
- 3 tablespoons tomato paste
- 1 tablespoon sweet paprika
- 1 teaspoon caraway seeds
- 1 pinch sugar
- 500 ml (2 cups/ 16 fl oz) beef broth
- Salt, to taste
- Black pepper to taste

To Serve

- 2 tablespoons fresh parsley leaves, finely chopped
- 4 tablespoons sour cream

Instructions

1. Wash the cabbage and remove the outer leaves. Quarter the cabbage through the stem, then use a sharp knife to cut out and discard the dense core.
2. Slice the cabbage into thin strips using a knife or a mandoline.
3. Finely chop the onions and mince the garlic.
4. In a large pot, heat the vegetable oil over medium-high heat. Add the ground beef and cook until it starts to brown, breaking it up with a spoon to crumble evenly and ensure there are no clumps.
5. Add the chopped onions and garlic to the browned beef and cook for another 5 minutes, stirring occasionally, until the onions are soft and fragrant.
6. Stir in the tomato paste and cook for 1 minute, allowing the flavors to develop.
7. Add the cabbage and briefly sauté with the beef, mixing well.
8. Deglaze the pot with beef broth, scraping up any browned bits from the bottom. Stir to combine.
9. Season generously with salt, black pepper, caraway seeds, paprika, and a pinch of sugar to balance the flavors.
10. Cover with a lid and simmer for 15 to 20 minutes, until the cabbage is tender but still has a slight bite. Stir occasionally.
11. Garnish with chopped parsley and serve with a dollop of sour cream for extra richness.

SERVING: 4 PEOPLE **PREP:** 15 MINS **COOK:** 1 HR 30 MINS

Szegediner Gulasch

Goulash with Sauerkraut

While this dish is actually Hungarian, it's also very popular in Germany. It has all the goodness of a slow-cooked goulash, with the added bonus of tangy sauerkraut and sour cream. Serve it with Semmelknödel (p. 33), Spätzle (p. 38), or boiled potatoes—and check out the recipe post on my blog if you want to learn more about its history.

Ingredients

- 1 kg (2 lb) pork, ideally from the shoulder (or use 500 g (1 lb) pork cubes and 500 g (1 lb) beef cubes), cubed
- 4 tablespoons vegetable oil
- 3 tablespoon all-purpose flour
- 500 g (1 lb) onions, roughly chopped
- 500 g (1 lb) sauerkraut (the exact taste will depend on which sauerkraut you use, such as German Weinsauerkraut. If your sauerkraut is very tangy, use less and adjust to taste).
- 1 teaspoon salt
- ½ teaspoon white pepper
- 1 teaspoon ground caraway seeds
- 1 teaspoon dried thyme
- 1 teaspoon marjoram (can be substituted with sage)
- 5 tablespoons ground sweet Hungarian paprika
- 2 garlic cloves, crushed
- 3 tablespoons tomato puree
- 500 ml (2 cups/ 17 fl oz) vegetable broth

To serve

- 100 g /3.5 oz sour cream (can be substituted with crème fraîche)
- 1 small bunch parsley, chopped

More info at https://mydinner.co.uk/goulash-and-sauerkraut-bake/ or Google "*MyDinner Goulash writh Sauerkraut*".

Szegediner Gulasch

Goulash with Sauerkraut

Instructions

1. Season the meat with salt and pepper.
2. Peel and roughly chop the onions. Crush the garlic. Drain the sauerkraut using a sieve.
3. Heat the oil in a large saucepan and brown the meat on all sides.
4. Sprinkle the flour over the meat and continue to brown, stirring continuously.
5. Add the onions and continue to sauté until they turn translucent. Reduce the heat and stir in the paprika. Be careful not to let the paprika burn, as it will turn bitter.
6. Add the salt, pepper, caraway seeds, thyme, marjoram, tomato puree, and garlic. Stir well and briefly fry with the meat and onions.
7. Pour in the vegetable broth, cover the pot with a lid, and simmer for 45 to 60 minutes on low heat.
8. Add the drained sauerkraut and mix with the meat. Cover the pot again and cook for an additional 30 minutes.
9. Serve with a dollop of sour cream and a sprinkle of fresh parsley. It is best to add the sour cream when serving, as reheating the goulash with sour cream mixed in may affect the texture.

More info at https://mydinner.co.uk/goulash-and-sauerkraut-bake/ or Google "*MyDinner Goulash writh Sauerkraut*".

Süsse Speisen und Nachtisch

SWEET TREATS AND DESSERTS

SERVING: 4 PEOPLE **PREP:** 5 MINS **COOK:** 30 MINS

Milchreis

Rice Pudding

Every bite of this creamy rice pudding takes me back to my childhood, when my mother would prepare it for lunch with some applesauce (p. 50) or cherry compote (p. 103). Every mouthful brought me one step closer to bliss. I like to add lemon zest to this dish—it gives the dish a zesty flavor that pairs beautifully with the warm vanilla tones.

Ingredients

For the rice pudding:

- 250 g (8.8 oz) short-grain rice *(such as rice pudding rice, arborio rice, sushi rice, or risotto rice)*
- 1 liter (4 cups / 34 fl oz) whole milk *(3.8% fat, or use another milk of your choice such as almond, soy, or oat milk)*
- 60 g (2 oz) granulated sugar (optional)
- 1 teaspoon grated lemon peel
- 1 pinch salt
- 1 vanilla bean (pulp only) or 1 teaspoon vanilla extract
- 1 tablespoon butter

Options for serving:

- 4 tablespoons sugar mixed with ground cinnamon
- Kirschgrütze (p. 103)
- Apple Sauce (p.50) or a fruit compote of your choice

Instructions

1. Add the rice, milk, sugar, grated lemon peel, and vanilla bean pulp or extract into a saucepan and bring to a boil.
2. Once boiling, reduce to low heat and simmer for 20 to 40 minutes, stirring continuously with a wooden spoon to prevent the bottom from burning. Cooking time may vary depending on the type of rice used. The Milchreis is ready when the rice is creamy and the grains are no longer crunchy, but tender.
3. In a separate pan, brown the butter. Once the rice is cooked, gently stir in the browned butter.
4. To serve, pour the rice pudding into bowls. Sprinkle with the sugar and cinnamon mixture or top with your preferred fruit compote or sauce.

More info at https://mydinner.co.uk/milchreis/ or Google "*MyDinner* Milchreis" .

SERVING: 4 PEOPLE **PREP:** 10 MINS **REST:** 30 MINS **COOK:** 15 MINS

Pfannkuchen

German Pancakes

Pfannkuchen, served with apple sauce (p. 50) and cinnamon sugar, were always the epitome of German comfort food. We do not serve them for breakfast, like the Americans and British, but for lunch. This is the recipe my mother always made for me, and I continue the tradition by still making it today for my children.

Ingredients

- 200 g (1 ½ cups or 7 oz) all-purpose flour
- 250 ml (1 cup or 8.4 fl oz) milk
- 4 eggs
- 60 ml (¼ cup or 2 fl oz) carbonated water/seltzer water
- 1 pinch of sugar
- 1 pinch of salt
- 80g (⅓ cup) butter for frying

Pancake Toppings

- 100 ml (⅓ cup) apple sauce (optional)
- Sugar and cinnamon mix (optional)
- Jam (optional)
- Chocolate spread (optional)

Instructions

1. In a large bowl, whisk together the flour and milk until the mixture is smooth and no lumps remain.
2. Add the eggs and continue whisking the batter.
3. Finally, add the sugar, salt, and carbonated water, then mix again until the batter is smooth and even.
4. Refrigerate the batter for at least 30 minutes. (This allows the gluten to develop, improving the pancake's texture.)
5. Heat the butter in a non-stick frying pan over medium heat. Once the butter melts and starts sizzling, use a ladle to pour the batter into the pan.
6. Cook the pancake until the bottom is set, which should take approximately 2 minutes. Then, flip the pancake and cook for another 2 minutes on the other side.
7. Remove the pancake, check if there is enough butter in the pan, then add another ladle of batter. Repeat the process until all the batter is used.

More info at https://mydinner.co.uk/pfannkuchen-recipe/ or Google "*MyDinner Pfannkuchen*" .

SERVING: 4 PEOPLE **PREP:** 10 MINS **COOK:** 15 MINS

Apfelpfannkuchen

Apple pancakes

Pancakes are unbeatable, unless you place some sliced apples into the batter and sprinkle cinnamon sugar on top. My Apfelpfannkuchen recipe is super fluffy, almost like American pancakes, the secret are the beaten egg whites.

Ingredients

- 225 g (1 cup/8 oz) all-purpose flour
- 3 medium eggs, at room temperature
- 180 ml (¾ cup / 6 fl oz) milk
- 60 ml (¼ cup / 2 fl oz) carbonated water (seltzer water)
- 1 pinch of salt
- 1 pinch of granulated sugar
- 4 apples
- 1 tablespoon lemon juice
- 4 teaspoons brown sugar
- 4 tablespoons butter or vegetable oil
- Cinnamon sugar, for serving

Instructions

1. Separate the eggs. Using a hand or stand mixer with a whisk attachment, beat the egg whites with a pinch of salt until stiff peaks form. Set aside.
2. In a large mixing bowl, combine the flour and milk, whisking until no lumps remain.
3. Add the egg yolks, carbonated water, sugar, and salt, mixing until a thick batter forms.
4. Carefully fold in the beaten egg whites, then refrigerate the mixture for approximately 30 minutes. (This resting period allows the gluten in the batter to develop, giving the pancake improved stability.)
5. In the meantime, core and slice the apples into thin wedges (approximately 0.5 cm / ¼ inch thick). Pour the lemon juice over them to prevent browning and sprinkle with brown sugar.
6. Heat butter or vegetable oil in a non-stick frying pan over medium-high heat. Once the butter melts and starts sizzling, use a ladle to pour the batter into the pan. (The batter is slightly thick, so you may need to spread it with a spoon.)
7. Arrange the apple slices in a circular pattern on top of the pancake batter.

More info at https://mydinner.co.uk/german-caramelised-apple-pancake/ or Google "*MyDinner Apple Pancakes*" .

Apfelpfannkuchen

German Apple Pancakes

8. Cook on low to medium heat for approximately 2–3 minutes. (Exact cooking times may vary. You will know the pancake is ready when you can easily lift the edges.)
9. To flip the pancake without breaking it, place a serving plate over the pan. Hold the plate firmly with one hand and flip the pan over with the other, allowing the plate to catch the pancake.
10. Place the pan back on the stove and slide the pancake back into the pan from the plate. Cook on the other side for another 2–3 minutes.
11. To serve, sprinkle the pancake with cinnamon sugar.

SERVING: 4 PEOPLE **PREP:** 10 MINS **COOK:** 20 MINS

Apfelküchle

Apple Fritters

Here's a recipe that will delight both adults and children! The first time I had these apple fritters was in a restaurant in Bayreuth, Bavaria. They were served with vanilla sauce (p. 98), and I instantly knew one serving wouldn't be enough. Since then, I've been making them for my family, and there are never any leftovers.

Ingredients

- 2 apples tart
- 1 tablespoon lemon juice (optional)
- 120 g (½ cup or 4.2 oz) all-purpose flour
- 1 teaspoon granulated sugar
- 1 pinch salt
- 2 medium eggs
- 120 ml (½ cup or 4 fl oz) milk or 120 ml (½ cup or 4 fl oz) beer
- 500 ml (2 cups or 17 fl oz) oil (Use an oil with a neutral taste, such as rapeseed oil or sunflower oil. Alternatively, you can also fry them in clarified butter for a buttery taste.)

Instructions

1. Peel the apples and remove the core using an apple corer or by cutting it out by hand. The hole should be about 2–3 cm (1 inch) wide.
2. Slice the apples into 1.5 cm (½ inch) thick rings. Squeeze lemon juice over them to prevent browning and set aside.
3. In a bowl, mix the flour, sugar, and salt. Add eggs and milk (or beer), then whisk until smooth.
4. Place apple rings into the batter, ensuring they are fully coated.
5. Using a deep saucepan or frying pan, heat oil to about 170°C (340°F).
6. If you don't have a cooking thermometer, test the oil with a wooden spoon. If bubbles form around it, the oil is ready.
7. Carefully place battered apple slices into hot oil and fry for about 3 minutes per side until crisp and golden.
8. Only fry a few rings at a time, as overcrowding may cause them to stick together.
9. Once fried, transfer to a kitchen towel to absorb excess oil.

SERVING: 4 PEOPLE **PREP:** 5 MINS **COOK:** 5 MINS

Vanillesoße

Vanilla Sauce

This dessert sauce is simple, elegant, and the perfect partner for so many German dishes. Whether on bread pudding (p. 99), Apelküchle (p. 98) or Rote Grütze (p. 104), this sauce is not going to disappoint.

Ingredients

- 500 ml (2 cups) milk
- 2 tablespoon cornstarch
- 3 tablespoon sugar
- 1 pinch salt
- 1 vanilla pod (or 2 teaspoons vanilla extract or vanilla sugar)
- 2 egg yolks

Instructions

1. In a small bowl, combine the cornstarch with 4 tablespoons of milk. Mix until you achieve a smooth paste without any lumps.
2. Add the remaining milk, salt, and sugar to a saucepan.
3. Slice the vanilla pod open lengthwise and scrape out the vanilla bean pulp. Add both to the milk mixture. *(Alternatively, mix in the vanilla extract or vanilla sugar.)*
4. Bring the milk mixture to a gentle boil, then remove the vanilla bean from the milk. *(Do not discard it—you can use it to make vanilla sugar.)*
5. While stirring continuously, pour in the cornstarch-milk mixture. Let it boil for one minute, then remove from heat.
6. In a separate bowl, combine 6 tablespoons of the hot milk mixture with the egg yolks and mix until well combined. *(This prevents the egg yolks from cooking too quickly when added to the sauce.)*
7. Lastly, pour the egg mixture into the rest of the sauce and stir well.

SERVING: 4 PEOPLE **PREP:** 10 MINS **COOK:** 29 MINS

Kirschmichel

Bread Pudding with Cherries

This recipe transforms stale bread into a lush, fruity dessert. I was never a big fan of bread pudding - but this dish convinced me otherwise. This Bavarian classic is named after cherries and a boy called Michael. Serve this classic dish with powdered sugar and warm vanilla sauce (p. 98)

Ingredients

- 500 g (1.1 lb) cherries (sour cherries or black cherries, defrosted or from a jar)
- 4 stale bread rolls (ideally from the day before, or use old baguette instead)
- 2 tablespoons breadcrumbs
- 300 ml (1 ¼ cups / 10 fl oz) warm milk
- 1 pinch salt
- 4 tablespoons butter (plus more for greasing the casserole dish)
- 100 g (1/2 cup) granulated sugar
- 3 medium eggs (at room temperature)
- 1 teaspoon vanilla extract
- 1 teaspoon almond extract
- 2 teaspoons baking powder
- Powdered sugar (for serving)

Instructions

1. Roughly cube the bread and pour warm milk over it. (The milk measurement is only a guide, as it depends on how old your bread rolls are.) The bread should soak up the liquid and soften without falling apart. Add more milk if needed.
2. Place the cherries in a strainer and drain off excess liquid.
3. Preheat oven to 200°C (390°F), using top-and-bottom heat.
4. Grease a casserole dish with butter, then sprinkle with breadcrumbs.
5. Separate the eggs. Whisk the egg whites with a pinch of salt until stiff peaks form.
6. In a separate bowl, mix the butter, sugar, baking powder, vanilla extract, almond extract, and egg yolks until smooth. Then, combine with the soaked bread mixture.
7. Carefully fold in the beaten egg whites. Be gentle, as overmixing may deflate them.
8. Add the cherries, then pour the mixture into the prepared casserole dish.
9. Bake for about 30 minutes.

More info at https://mydinner.co.uk/bread-pudding/ or Google "*MyDinner Bread Pudding*".

SERVING: 8 PEOPLE **PREP:** 20 MINS **COOK:** 15 MINS

Herzwaffeln

Heart-Shaped Waffles

Homemade waffles are one of my fondest childhood memories. They're served at Christmas markets, school festivals, and I often make them as a quick treat for my children during their playdates. You can make these waffles in a heart-shaped waffle maker, but a rectangular Belgian-style machine works just as well.

Ingredients

- 250 g (1 cup/9 oz) unsalted butter, softened
- 200 g (1 cup/7 oz) granulated sugar
- 1 pinch salt
- 1 teaspoon vanilla extract
- 5 medium eggs, at room temperature
- 500 g (4 cups/18 oz) all-purpose flour
- 2 teaspoons baking powder
- 500 ml (2.5 cups/17 fl oz) whole milk

Instructions

1. To avoid a lumpy waffle batter, make sure that all the ingredients are at room temperature. If your butter is too cold, gently warm it in the microwave for a few seconds.
2. Place the butter, sugar, salt, and vanilla extract in a bowl. Beat with a hand mixer, stand mixer, or whisk for about 5 minutes until light and creamy.
3. Add the eggs one at a time, beating well after each addition.
4. In a separate bowl, mix the flour and baking powder. Gradually add this to the wet ingredients, alternating with the milk. Mix until you get a smooth, fluffy batter.
5. Heat your waffle maker. Once it reaches the desired temperature, lightly grease the plates with a little butter to prevent the waffles from sticking.
6. Pour in a scoop of batter and cook the waffles until golden brown.

More info at https://mydinner.co.uk/basic-recipe-german-waffles/ or Google "*MyDinner German Waffles*".

SERVING: 12 DONUTS **PREP:** 10 MINS **COOK:** 20 MINS **REST:** 2 HRS

Berliner

Jam Donuts

These beloved jam donuts are a bit of an obsession in Germany. You will find them at every bakery. They are known by different names, depending on the region in Germany you are in: Berliner, Krepple. Krapfen und Berliner Pfannkuchen. It is about time to make these sugary treats at home.

Ingredients

For the Dough:

- 200 ml (¾ cup | 6.7 fl oz) lukewarm milk
- 70 g (2 ½ oz) butter, at room temperature
- 500 g (17 2/3 oz | 4 cups) flour (Germany: Type 405, UK: plain flour, US: pastry flour)
- 40 g (3 tablespoons) sugar
- 1 teaspoon vanilla extract
- ½ teaspoon salt
- 7 g (1/4 oz | 1 packet or 2 teaspoons) instant yeast
- 3 egg yolks

For the Filling:

- 250 g (¾ cup) jam

For Frying:

- 750 ml (3 cups) vegetable oil (such as sunflower oil). Alternatively, use vegetarian lard.

Instructions

1. In a small bowl, mix the sugar and yeast into the lukewarm milk. Leave to stand for about 10 minutes. The yeast should start to bubble.
2. Add the flour, butter, vanilla extract, and salt to a large bowl. Pour in the yeast mixture and knead into a thick dough using a stand or hand mixer.
3. Add the egg yolks one at a time, then knead the dough for about 5 minutes.
4. Place the dough in a lightly greased bowl (to prevent sticking) and cover it with a kitchen towel. Leave to rise for about 1 hour (preferably in a warm spot).
5. Knead the risen dough with your hands on a lightly floured surface. Then divide the dough into 12 even pieces. (Each should weigh approximately 60 g (2 oz).)
6. Shape each piece into a ball:
   - Using a circular motion with the palm of your hand, gently roll the dough on a floured surface to create a round shape.
   - Alternatively, roll the dough between both palms using the same circular motion.

Berliner

Jam Donuts

7. The dough balls will enlarge during the final rising period.
8. Place the dough balls on a lined baking tray and cover them with a tea towel. Leave to rise for another 3 minutes.

Frying the Donuts

1. Heat the oil in a large pot. Use a thermometer and allow the temperature to rise to 170°C (338°F).
2. If you do not have a thermometer, test the oil by placing a wooden spoon in it. If bubbles form around the spoon, the oil is ready. Reduce the heat slightly.
3. It is important not to fry the donuts at too high a temperature, as this will cause them to cook unevenly. They may also cook too quickly on the outside, while remaining undercooked in the center.
4. Fry each donut for approximately 3 minutes per side, or until golden brown.
5. Remove the donuts with a slotted spoon and place them on a kitchen towel to absorb excess grease.
6. Let the donuts cool for at least 20 minutes before filling.

Filling the Donuts

1. Fill a piping bag with the jam of your choice. (If your jam contains fruit pieces, strain it through a sieve to prevent clogging the piping tip.)
2. Use a long, narrow nozzle (approximately 7 millimeters) to fill each donut.
3. Dust each donut with powdered sugar before serving.

More info at https://mydinner.co.uk/berliner-donut/ or Google "*MyDinner Berliner Donuts*".

SERVING: 12 DONUTS **PREP:** 5 MINS **COOK:** 5 MINS

Kirschgrütze

Cherry Compote

If you ask me, making this sour cherry compote is always a good idea. There's no need to wait for cherry season—frozen or canned cherries work just as well. It's a popular topping for waffles, pancakes, or yogurt. My children also enjoy it on its own, topped with a drizzle of vanilla sauce *(p. 98)**.*

Ingredients

- 500 g (1 lb) cherries – use fresh pitted cherries, canned cherries, or frozen cherries (defrosted)
- 500 ml (2 cups) water – if using canned cherries, you can use the juice from the jar
- 45 g (3 tablespoons) cornstarch (also known as cornflour) – use less if you prefer a thinner compote, more for a thicker consistency
- 50 g (4 tablespoons) sugar – adjust according to taste
- 1 teaspoon vanilla extract

Instructions

1. Drain the jar of cherries, making sure to reserve the juice.
2. Add enough water to the juice until you have 500 ml (2 cups) of liquid. (If using frozen cherries, use water instead.)
3. Remove 90 ml (6 tablespoons) of the liquid and mix it with the cornstarch, sugar, and vanilla extract in a bowl to form a thick paste. Stir or whisk until no clumps remain.
4. In a saucepan, heat the cherries over medium heat until they begin to boil.
5. Stir in the cornstarch paste and boil for 2 minutes, until the cherry sauce thickens.
6. Serve warm or let cool before storing.

SERVING: 4 PEOPLE **PREP:** 5 MINS **REST:** 2 HOURS **COOK:** 10 MINS

Rote Grütze

Red Berry Pudding

This refreshing dish tastes of summer. It is a berry dessert from Northern Germany. A quick, not-too-sweet treat that everybody loves. Serve it with vanilla sauce (p. 98) or pudding. It also tastes great as a sauce on top of waffles or cheesecake.

Ingredients

- 500 g (1 lb) mixed berries, fresh or frozen (e.g., raspberries, red currants, strawberries, red berries)
- 2 teaspoons vanilla extract
- 3 tablespoons cornstarch (or cornflour)
- 3 tablespoons granulated sugar
- 300 ml (1 ¼ cups) water
- 1 jar sour cherry Morello cherries (680 g / 23 oz), optional (or substitute with frozen cherries)

Instructions

1. If using fresh berries, wash them thoroughly, remove any stems, and halve the strawberries.
2. Divide the berries (fresh or frozen) into two equal portions.
3. If using sour cherries, strain them and reserve the juice in a separate glass.
4. In a small bowl, mix 3 tablespoons of the reserved cherry juice (or water, if not using cherries) with the cornstarch. Stir until smooth and free of lumps.
5. In a medium saucepan, combine one portion of the berries, the sugar, and the vanilla extract. Add the water (or the remaining cherry juice, if using) and bring to a boil over medium heat. Cook for about 5 minutes, or until the fruit starts to break down.
6. Remove the saucepan from the heat and puree the mixture using a blender or immersion blender until smooth.
7. Return the pureed mixture to the stove over medium heat. Stir the cornstarch slurry again to ensure it's smooth, then slowly pour it into the berry mixture while stirring continuously. Bring the mixture to a boil, then reduce the heat and simmer for about 5 minutes, stirring constantly, until thickened.
8. Stir in the second portion of berries and, if using, the sour cherries. Mix until well combined.
9. Allow the mixture to cool to room temperature. Then transfer it to the refrigerator and chill for at least 2 hours before serving.

SERVING: 4 PEOPLE **PREP:** 15 MINS **COOK:** 45 MINS

Bratapfel

Baked Apples with Cinnamon and Nuts

When the days start to turn colder, nothing beats this comforting Bratapfel dessert. Apples stuffed with nuts, cinnamon, and sugar, then slowly baked to perfection. Use red-colored apples for the prettiest result. Serve with ice cream or vanilla sauce (p.38)

Ingredients

- 4 large tart apples, such as Boskoop, Elstar, Jonagold, Granny Smith, Braeburn, Honeycrisp, or Bramley apples
- 60 g (4 tablespoons) raisins or currants
- 30 ml (2 tablespoons) rum (optional, can be omitted)
- 50 g (1.7 oz) chopped nuts, such as almonds, hazelnuts, or walnuts
- 30 g (2 tablespoons) butter
- 15 g (1 tablespoon) brown sugar
- 15 ml (1 tablespoon) lemon juice
- 2.5 g (½ teaspoon) ground cinnamon (use more if desired)
- Choose one:
- 50 g (1.7 oz) marzipan
- 45 g (3 tablespoons) fruit jam (use a slightly sour jam such as apricot, cherry, or red currant jam)

Instructions

Preparing the Filling

1. Soak the raisins or currants in rum overnight if desired. (This step is optional.)
2. Place the nuts in a frying pan over medium heat and roast them, stirring constantly to prevent burning.
3. Once the nuts become fragrant and start to brown gently, add the butter and brown sugar.
4. Stir until the sugar dissolves and the nuts caramelize. Remove the pan from the heat and stir in the raisins or currants, ground cinnamon, and lemon juice.
5. Add the marzipan to the warm nuts. Knead everything together to form a smooth paste. (The heat will soften the marzipan, making it easier to work with.) Alternatively, if using jam instead of marzipan, mix to form a smooth paste.

Bratapfel

Baked Apples with Cinnamon and Nuts

Preparing the Apples

1. Preheat your oven to 180°C (356°F) convection heat. Lightly grease the bottom of a baking dish with butter.
2. Carefully slice off the top of each apple. Using an apple corer or a sharp knife, carve out the center of the apple. (Make the hole slightly larger to allow enough space for the filling.)
3. Place the apple bottoms into the baking dish. Fill each apple with the marzipan or jam mixture using a spoon. To prevent air pockets, gently press down the filling with the handle of a wooden spoon.
4. Place the apple tops back on (optional, but adds a nice touch).
5. Bake the apples for about 45 minutes. Halfway through the baking time, loosely cover them with aluminum foil to prevent burning or over-browning.

MAKE SURE TO CHECK ALSO MY CHRISTMAS BAKING RECIPES COOKBOOK!

THANK YOU!

WWW.MYDINNER.CO.UK

@MYDINNER.CO.UK

@MYDINNERS

9781806540440
20250904000833

Made in Canada by LoginPOD
Powered by Publishers' Graphics
loginpod.ca
PGCA2024